Victorious Exile

The Unexpected Destiny of Katya Kolyschkine

by Echo Lewis

Catherine de Hueck Doherty's amazing
journey through loss, love, death,
and resurrection.

D1121271

Madonna House Publications
Combermere, Ontario, Canada

 Madonna House Publications
2888 Dafoe Rd, RR 2
Combermere, Ontario
Canada KOJ 1LO
www.madonnahouse.org/publications

Victorious Exile: The Unexpected Destiny of Katya Kolyschkine
Catherine de Hueck Doherty's Amazing Journey through loss, love, death and resurrection
by Echo Lewis

First edition: February 2nd, 2013

Layout Design: Rosalie Douthwright
Cover Design: Rob Huston

Library and Archives Canada Cataloguing in Publication

Lewis, Echo
     Victorious exile : the unexpected destiny of Katya Kolyschkine :
Catherine de Hueck Doherty's amazing journey into loss, love, death and
resurrection / Echo Lewis.

Includes bibliographical references.
ISBN 978-1-897145-37-1

     1. Doherty, Catherine de Hueck, 1896-1985. 2. Catholics--Biography.
I. Title.

BX4705.D56L49 2013   282.092   C2012-908133-7

Printed in Canada

Dedication

For Theresa Davis, Linda Lambeth, and Fr. David May,
who walked every step of the way with me

And in memory of my sister Vicki, who, in the special
exile that illness brings, felt a close kinship with Katya

Author's Note

Katya Kolyschkine was a storyteller. She once told me, "If there's one gift God has given me, it's the gift of words."

Katya absorbed a great deal of her Russian history and traditions from stories handed down through the oral tradition of her ancestors. Later, as an exile in Canada and America, she introduced Russian culture to Westerners through stories. It was her favorite way of communicating the deepest truths of human existence.

In keeping with that tradition, I have written Katya's biography in story form. Even so, all the facts are solid. All the words attributed to her are hers—taken from stories she told us in the dining room of Madonna House or from her diaries, letters, lectures, unpublished writings, tapes, books, articles, and interviews.

The Selected Bibliography at the back of the book contains almost all of the sources used in writing Katya's story.

Acknowledgements

A thousand thanks go to Bonnie Staib, for her multi-faceted support over the ten years it took to research and write this work.

Special thanks also go to Pat Broderick, Mark Lerch and Richard Peck for their advice and creative criticisms throughout the course of this project.

A huge note of gratitude goes to the teams at Madonna House Publications and Madonna House Archives for their help in getting this book into print, and to Surry Roberts for his steadfast encouragement and support.

When one lives in a community with a promise of poverty and a mandate to beg like St. Francis for all one's needs, one discovers the necessity of depending on others for everything from copy paper to a place of work. I remain ever grateful for the generous help of so many brothers and sisters, friends and benefactors in the Madonna House Apostolate in Raleigh, North Carolina, and beyond, especially:

Robin Biggie, Ellen Curro, JoAnne DeGidio, Maria de Souza, Posie Douthwright, Lorene Hanley Duquin for an abundance of valuable research, Cathy Foley, Jean Fox, RIP, Réjeanne George, The "Grupo" ladies and their families and friends, Jim Guinan RIP, Marian Heiberger, Beth Holmes, Serena Jones, Anne Killion, Paul Mackan, Sandra and David Malkovsky, Reggie Matthews, Fr. Pat McNulty, Dan McQuillen, Joan and Jacques Mistro, Mary Beth Mitchell, Marian Moody, Mary Nadeau whose request set the gears in motion, Rich Reid RIP, Mary Catherine Rowland, Gretchen Schafer, Michael Staszewski, Bob Staib, Monsignor John Williams, and Chris Zakrzewski.

Russian Cast of Characters

(Including Names, Nicknames, English equivalents, and some pronunciation aids)

Ekaterina (Katya) Kolyschkine (Ee-cat-er-éena Cóal-ish-kin): later known in the West as Catherine de Hueck, Catherine Doherty, Katie, and the B

Fyodor Kolyschkine (Theodore): Katya's father

Emma Kolyschkine: Katya's mother

Serge Kolyschkine: Katya's younger brother by seven years

Andrew Kolyschkine: Katya's youngest brother by sixteen years

Vsevolod (Volya) Kolyschkine: Katya's older stepbrother by sixteen years

Boris (Borya) de Hueck: Katya's cousin and later her husband, seven years older than she

Guido de Hueck: Boris's father and Katya's uncle by marriage, later Katya's father-in-law

Vera (Kolyschkine) de Hueck: Fyodor's sister, Boris's mother and Katya's aunt, later Katya's mother-in-law

Nikolai (Nicholas) Effreinoff: Vera's second husband and Boris's stepfather

Nicholas (Kolya) Makletzoff: Russian soldier and friend of Katya

Martha Van Schraam: Guido de Hueck's second wife and mother of Boris's two young stepbrothers, George and Paul

George de Hueck (Russian by nationality, Canadian by birth): Katya's and Boris's son

Contents

Prologue

*B*ack home in Russia, everybody had called Katya the strong one. But now, constant hunger made her weak and dizzy. She stumbled out of the British Red Cross building. Damp tendrils of her long blonde hair escaped from the knot piled on top of her head and clung to her temples. She shivered in the chill of London's autumn evening air.

Katya earned one shilling for sitting all day at a treadle machine stitching underwear for soldiers. For the reward of a second shilling, she had started doing overtime. Today, she had made it to the end only by sheer will power.

She trudged toward the nearest bus stop. Before she could reach it, the dizziness overtook her. She braced herself against the wall of a perfumery. If she ate the hardboiled egg she'd saved from lunch, she might make it all the way to the YMCA.

No. Boris needed the egg more than she did. She took a slow, deep breath. In that still moment, she glanced through the perfumery window. A tall Englishwoman with a fur draped over her shoulders was inhaling the scent of what looked like an exotic bottle of perfume. Katya balled her hand into a fist. She could feed Boris for two months on what that perfume must cost!

Frightened at the force of her rage, Katya swung away and ran to the next bus stop. At the "Y", her anger propelled her up the long sets of stairs to the attic. She had nothing; and her husband lay sick with damaged lungs and shell shock.

Katya flung open the door to their room. Seeing Boris so pale and still under the thin blanket drained the anger from her. She drew the cover higher over his sleeping form, and wondered for the hundredth time at the horrific series of events that had cast her into this foreign country. She had to struggle as hard to survive here as she had in the War and Revolution. Would the days ahead be worse than the ones from which they had just escaped?

Katya in England, recovering from her war experiences

Chapter 1

A Pilgrim's Prophecy

*Born rich, beautiful, and brilliant, Katya Kolysch-
kine should have been destined for a life of frivolous
comfort and ease. So, when her mother held her
new baby in her arms, why did she say she was born
under the sign of the cross?*

Katya's parents: Emma and
Fyodor Kolyschkine

*K*atya jumped at the sudden knock on the front door
of the Kolyschkine's Tambov farmhouse. In the
yellow light of the wall lantern, she
watched her father Fyodor get up
from his place at the head of the
long wooden supper table.

At first, Katya could only see his
tall, thin frame in the doorway.
When he stepped aside to let the
visitor enter, the flickering lantern
light caught the craggy features of
an old woman covered in fresh snow.
She shook away the gathered flakes;
and Katya saw that she wore an icon

of the Virgin Mary and Jesus, hanging from a cord around her neck.

Katya knew all about the pilgrims who roamed deep in the forests and across the vast steppes of her early twentieth-century Holy Russia. They strove to preserve God's peace and love in a land ravaged by inequality and centuries of sorrow from invasion, war, and famine. Content to live in poverty, these pilgrims begged for food and lodging wherever they could find them.

Russian Pilgrim

"Would you be so kind," this woman asked in the crinkly voice of the very old, "as to shelter one who has had an experience well beyond the ordinary?"

Katya caught her breath. She was in for a good story.

When the old woman finished her bread and soup, the servants and their children joined the Kolyschkines at the table. To the accompaniment of the crackling logs burning in the fireplace, the pilgrim began to speak.

"I entered the great forest near here," she confided in a hoarse whisper. "Dusk gave way to darkness; and I became uneasy.

"As I walked, I heard the trees rustling. They whispered among themselves about the closeness of the Evil One. Wild forest creatures started to run away and hide. I began blessing myself with the sign of the Cross.

"A man fell into step beside me.

"'Hello, Granny,' he said in a quiet tone that sent a chill down my back.

"He talked about how our people are poor and exploited, and how Christianity isn't the answer to our problems. Before I knew it, I found his words making sense.

"Then the man made a mistake. He mocked us who believe that the Blessed Mother gave birth to the Lord and remained a virgin. That's when I knew!

"Quietly, I took out my little bottle of holy water. In the dark, the man couldn't see what I was doing. I sprinkled him with it in the name of Jesus and in the name of the Holy Trinity. The man screamed, twisted, and fell on the ground—then vanished. But before he vanished, he cried out,

"'You old fool! All Russia will be covered with rivers of blood over the things I've told you. Millions will think like I do. There will be moaning and tears all over this land. I am out to win it, and win it I will. Neither you nor your God nor your Blessed Virgin will be able to save it.'

"So terrible were his words and his voice that I fell senseless to the ground. When I awoke, I started walking, terrified, out of the forest.

"Suddenly there was a great light on the road; and a young woman came up to my side.

"'Fear not, Grandma,' she said. 'It is true what the man told you; but he was not a man. These things will come to pass so that Holy Russia may hang on the cross with my Son to redeem the world. The only way the world can be redeemed is through suffering with my Son. Fear not. There will come a day when, under the sign of the Cross, I will lead Russia to show my Son's face to the world.'

"Then she vanished too, and I saw the light of your windows."

The dying flames flickered less frequently now in the fireplace; and Katya trembled in the growing darkness.

After a long silence, Fyodor thanked the wizened pilgrim for sharing her story.

"We are blessed to have you stay with us as long as you wish," he said. "You may sleep over the oven." He indicated the customary warm shelf reserved for guests. He picked up Katya's sleeping baby brother Serge, bade everyone present a peaceful night, and made the Sign of

Katya and her brother Serge

the Cross on Katya's forehead. He and Katya's mother Emma then retreated to their room.

The servants and their children drifted away too; and Katya found herself alone with the old pilgrim.

Katya at 7 or 8 years old

"Goldilocks," the ancient one said, touching Katya's blonde curls, "you will be married twice, but your Spouse is eternal. You have been chosen by Him for His work. Don't try to escape."

Bewildered, Katya climbed the narrow stairs to her low-ceilinged bedroom loft. She lay awake a long time, starting at every strange noise, and wondering what sort of work the old pilgrim had thought God wanted her to do.

Chapter 2

Storm Clouds Gather

"This is the last bauble for a long time."
(Katya's father to her mother)

Katya, her parents and chauffeur, Egypt, 1905

For a while, Katya fretted over the ancient one's prophecy. But then the Christmas holiday in Russia ended, and Katya went back to Egypt. Lloyd's of Russia Insurance Company had assigned her father to manage a branch office in Alexandria, and Katya attended a grade school in the suburb of Ramleh, run by the English Sisters of Sion. Class work, playing with her friends, and a Spring Break trip with her family to the Holy Land for Easter pushed the pilgrim's prediction into a hazy memory.

By the time spring rolled into summer, and Katya returned to Tambov, her mother provided something else to occupy her thoughts. Emma declared that it was time for Katya to join her in "going to the people." At a peasant's two-room *izba*, set in a small forest village, Emma allowed Katya to scrub the floor, wash dishes, and watch the children while she tended to the sick woman.

As she worked, Katya wondered how people could live in such a dark, damp hut. Why couldn't they afford to call a doctor?

Her mother explained that the rural peasants and city laborers usually got such poor wages that they couldn't take proper care of their families. Hunger, exhaustion from their grueling work schedules, and humiliation sometimes drove them to rebel against the Tsar and his government.

Katya in Egypt

Who could blame the peasants for being angry, Katya thought. Russia needed more people like St. Francis of Assisi. The Sisters in Ramleh had introduced Katya to the thirteenth-century friar who was so kind that even the wild animals grew tame near him. Katya decided that, when she could, she would do what St. Francis did—sell everything she had and give the money to those who needed it. She would be like her mother, too, and go to the poor to help them.

In 1908, when Katya turned twelve, she wrote in her diary,

"One must be always charitable and feed the hungry and give to the poor, but what can I give? All belongs to Mother."

Katya's philosophical thoughts got interrupted when her life took an unexpected turn. Lloyd's of Russia ran into hard times; and Katya's father had to close the office in Alexandria.

Reveling in the sheer drama of it, Katya looked on in awe as her father presented her mother with a diamond necklace, saying, "This is the last bauble for a long time. We're in financial ruin."

Sorry to leave her school and the Sisters, but excited about setting off on a new adventure, Katya helped pack the family belongings for a move to Paris. Fyodor had been offered a humble position there with the same insurance company.

Katya liked the little French apartment on a side street of the big city. She already knew some French, and before long, she could haggle over vegetable prices at the street market with the most vocal merchants. Rubbing shoulders with the throngs of other shoppers—peasants, laborers, and lowly city clerks—Katya concluded that financial ruin suited her.

She didn't get to enjoy financial ruin for long. Soon after she entered her 'teens, Katya moved with her family back home to Russia's capital city of St. Petersburg. Lloyd's of Russia had regained its financial stability, and Fyodor had been named the manager

Peter the Great: "The Bronze Horseman"

of an international office. It was a significant move for Katya, who entered Princess Obolensky Gymnasium (high school), and picked up the thread of her musings about the meaning of life for herself and those around her.

The Kolyschkine's St. Petersburg home, the entire third floor, 25 Morskaya Street

She leaned on the railing of her family's flat and thought about poverty and wealth. Her father had run into financial ruin for a while, but he hadn't lost his ancestral home. It covered the entire third floor of the block-long building at 25 Morskaya Street, and had nineteen rooms—the same number as the islands that made up the whole of St. Petersburg. Her older stepbrother Vsevolod, his wife Lyusya, and their five children had come to live with them. Even so, the flat wasn't crowded. She and her family had all they needed, and more.

Others had so little. She felt sorry for them; but like St. Francis, Leo Tolstoy, her favorite author, wrote that because the poor had to depend entirely on God for everything, they had a special place in His heart. So, shouldn't people want to be poor?

Sighing, Katya looked out over the city. The clear autumn sunlight glanced off the golden dome of their church, St. Isaac's Russian Orthodox Cathedral, and off the network of canals and bridges that criss-crossed the "Venice of the North".

Boat on one of the many St. Petersburg canals

She loved so much about this beautiful city. Russia's most universally beloved poet, Alexander Pushkin, had lived here. The ballets and operas she had to attend as part of her schooling thrilled her. The music of Nikolai Rimsky-Korsakov and the singing of Fyodor Chaliapin dazzled her imagination. At one of her mother's evening cultural gatherings, she met the painter Ilya Repin, whose representation of Ivan the Terrible killing his son made her gasp at the powerful portrayal of the first Tsar's madness. And yet, all that beauty and culture couldn't make up for the fact that the peasants and workers still received terrible treatment here and throughout her country. Maybe when she got older, it would all make more sense.

Katya didn't know it yet, but the struggle of Russia's poor and her own struggles in growing up were about to cascade into a single irreversible battle between good and evil.

Nevsky Prospect (the Avenue of the Tsars), St. Petersburg

St. Isaac's Cathedral

Chapter 3

Boris

"Promises made on sea are not kept on land."

(Russian Proverb)

℘lissfully ignorant of what was to come, Katya lived out the joys of her present life in St. Petersburg. She adored her stepbrother Vsevolod, whom everyone called Volya. Sixteen years older than she, he was the son of Fyodor and his first wife Ekaterina, who died when he was born. It wasn't until sixteen years later that Fyodor met and married Katya's mother Emma.

Boris de Hueck as a small boy with his father Guido de Hueck

For Katya, Volya was the most exciting person in her life—until her cousin Boris de Hueck started coming around to visit Volya. At twenty-one, Boris was midway between Katya and Volya in age. He studied architecture and engineering in the port city of Riga. His mother, Fyodor's sister Vera, lived in St. Petersburg;

and whenever Boris came home to visit her and his step-father Nikolai Effreinoff, he connected with Volya. The two cousins spent unlimited weekend hours partying in the city. Like plenty of other young men of the aristocracy, they seemed to find social irresponsibility a splendid way of life.

To Katya, Boris appeared grown-up and sophisticated. He didn't pay her much attention until, one day he stopped her in the hallway.

"You're beautiful," he said, and pulled her behind the library door for a hidden kiss.

In a matter of seconds, Katya's panoramic musings about the plight of the poor shifted to thoughts and dreams about only one other person on earth.

Volya (L) and Boris as boys

Katya had almost always been happy—so much so that her family and friends had dubbed her "Miss Laughter". This experience with Boris,

Katya's older half brother Vsevolod (Volya) (R), his and Katya's father Fyodor (C) and a friend (L)

though, promised something beyond the simple laughter of a child.

The only thing from the outside that broke into Katya's enchantment with Boris was the death of her hero, Leo Tolstoy. A born aristocrat, but champion of the poor, he had become old and sick. Knowing he was dying, he tore himself away from his comfortable home and, silently declaring his true alliance with the poor, boarded a train to nowhere, and died alone at a forsaken wayside station.

The country's downtrodden peasants and workers, along with revolutionaries of all sorts, saw Tolstoy's last act of turning away from a position of privilege to identify with the poor as a symbolic act of social rebellion. Student demonstrations broke out all across the country. For fourteen-year-old Katya, her grief over Tolstoy's death soon gave way to a renewed all-encompassing fixation on her cousin Boris. She felt her father's disapproval, but figured it was partly due to his grievance against Boris's father.

Fyodor declared that his feud with Guido de Hueck had nothing to do with his concern for Katya. He told her she was too young to know what she was doing, and forbade her to see Boris anymore.

Katya fought back. She said that if her father sent Boris away, she would follow him. If he sent her away, she said, Boris would come after her.

At last, her father relented. He stated that Katya would be formally engaged on her fifteenth birthday, and, at an appropriate time after that, she and Boris would marry.

Greatly excited at having won the battle, Katya helped her mother draw up guest lists and design her wedding dress.

Chapter 4

The Ill-Fated Doll Collection

"The road from the peak can lead only to the valley."

(Russian proverb)

*I*n spite of fleeting misgivings about her upcoming responsibilities as a married woman, Katya walked on clouds down the aisle of a side chapel in St. Isaac's Cathedral. The whipping January winds of 1912 couldn't harm a single thread of her hand-stitched gown or lace veil. Being a bride, and especially being the center of a great deal of attention, made it a grand event.

After the ceremony, Katya left the Cathedral in a horse-drawn sleigh, riding through the snowy streets with Boris to nearby 25 Morskaya Street. Attending to her duties as a new bride, she circulated among friends and family members, speaking—graciously, she hoped—to each one. She drank a glass of champagne and, like everyone else, threw her empty glass into a big wicker basket in front of the fireplace.

Later, in her room, as Katya changed into her matching royal-blue dress and hat for travel, she confronted a churning tangle of thoughts.

Fyodor and Guido's animosity toward each other had erupted when Boris was twelve years old. His father left his first wife, Fyodor's sister Vera, and eventually married his mistress, Martha Van Schraam. Because of the ensuing feud, Boris's mother and her second husband Nikolai, a retired army officer, were the only ones at the wedding or reception from Boris's side of the family. That hurt.

Then there was her mother's ominous warning.

"Don't expect Boris to be faithful to you," Emma had said in a quiet moment when the two had been alone.

Katya's head reeled as she packed the last of her Russian doll collection into her suitcase. Would Boris kiss other girls the way he kissed her? There was the time he and Lyusya had run away together, but even Tsar Nicholas II had had such girlfriends before he married Tsarina Alexandra. Now that Boris was married, surely he would be hers alone, wouldn't he?

With no answers to her questions, Katya picked up her suitcase, left her bedroom, and walked into her new life.

At first, she enjoyed Riga. An important Russian commercial and industrial center situated on the sandy plains of both banks of the Dvina River, it housed the de Hueck ancestral home—a string of medieval houses connected one to the other. Inside, dozens of de Hueck portraits dating back to the early eighteenth century lined the walls of a maze of corridors. Tsar Peter the Great had brought the first de Huecks from Holland to build his ships. Now, Boris's father owned several cotton mills and had his hand in a number of other businesses.

Guido and the rest of the current de Huecks had made their statement by not attending Katya and Boris's wedding, but now, Katya knew, they were obliged to receive her into the family. Soon after her arrival in Riga, she acted as hostess for a party Boris threw for all of his relatives. One of his aunts wandered into Katya's bedroom, and discovered her dolls. The woman brandished the dolls before everyone, to show what a silly child Boris had married.

Crimson with rage, Boris turned on Katya. She snatched up the dolls and fled from the room in tears.

It didn't take long for things to get worse. Katya had learned from her mother how to do all the kinds of work the servants did. "So you will know what's involved when

Girl with doll collection. Early 20th century postcard

asking someone to do a job," Emma had told her. It was rare training for a girl of Katya's position, but in Riga, she put it to more use than she could have wished. Boris attended classes, and made her spend long days cooking, cleaning, and mending. He demanded excellence in all of her work. When he came home from school, he made her do his homework of detailed technical drawings. When she made a mistake, he forced her to do the drawing over and over until she got it right. Sometimes, when she saw him coming, she hid under the bed.

In the fall of 1912, Boris finished the formal part of his studies; and he and Katya moved back to St. Petersburg. They set up house in an apartment on Geslerovsky Street, where Boris's father owned the building. In their new home, Boris made Katya continue her schedule of housework, done to his demanding standards. Meanwhile, he took up astronomy, and spent endless hours computing the distance between stars.

Katya managed to steal time from her housework to consume books by the dozens. Her voracious reading on every topic from philosophy and theology to the art of landscape painting angered Boris. Trying, as always, to please him and not incur his wrath, she put away her books whenever she saw him coming. As soon as he turned his back, she picked them up again. Seeing that he couldn't stop her from seeking knowledge, Boris organized a program of studies, and tutored her himself.

Besides studying, Katya discovered another pleasure. She liked being rich. As the wife of an aristocrat, she attended balls and sold trinkets at charity bazaars. She went shopping and got her hair done in the exclusive establishments along Nevsky Prospect, the long, doubly wide "Avenue of the Tsars." Her childhood dream of becoming poor like St. Francis of Assisi went into hiding.

In March, 1913, Katya's mother gave birth to a new baby boy named Andrew. Immersed in the luxuries that wealth bought and the joy of new life, Katya didn't take heed of the ever-expanding political shadow that spread all over Europe.

Chapter 5

War

"War is in the Tsar's hands, peace in God's."
(Russian proverb)

When war broke out between Russia and Germany in August, 1914, Boris joined the Corps of Imperial Engineers as a Major at the Northern Front. The following summer, eighteen-year-old Katya entered the escalating world war as a nurse's aide.

One evening, not long after she arrived at the same camp in which Boris was stationed, Katya stepped inside the nurses' tent, and saw their young helper struggling to break free from a drunken soldier. Katya lunged at the man. She tore him away from the girl, threw him to the ground, and jumped on him. A tooth fell from his mouth. He lurched to his feet; and Katya pummeled him with her fists. She heaved him out the door, and shouted after him,

"You filthy swine! I'll have you shot for this!"

Within minutes, the soldier stumbled back inside the tent. He threw himself at Katya's feet.

"Mercy!" he pleaded with a lisp. "My mother! My little sisters! They'll starve without my help. I was drunk—not myself. Have mercy!"

"Go!" Katya bellowed. "But if you ever . . ."

The soldier grabbed the hem of Katya's skirt, kissed it, and limped away.

Katya shuddered at the sight of the bloodstain he had left on her skirt, and wondered from what Tartar ancestor she had inherited that strength and fury.

Soon, Katya made more discoveries about herself. Three and a half years of living with Boris had left her with the impression that she had no value; but she found out she had a gift for organization. This quality and the ability to make her naturally deep voice heard over the din of mealtime clamor in the open fields landed her the added job of being head of the soup kitchen.

Late one morning, Katya and her cooking assistants drove their horse-drawn cauldron to a designated trench area. She let most of the assistants drive on through the

Silhouette of Russian soldiers at the Front, 1915

trenches, dispensing rations to the hungry troops. She and two helpers climbed onto the area platform, a high-rise floor that could open and close. Fish soup bubbled in a big iron pot. The sun rose toward noon, and Katya shaded her eyes to watch the peaceful distribution of soup, bread, and tea.

Suddenly, German shells exploded close to the ground. Shrapnel flew in all directions, killing, wounding, and tearing through the outpost.

"Dive!" Katya's two helpers cried, and scrambled down the ladder to hide under the platform.

"Get back here, you cowards!" Katya bellowed—and ran to the soup pot for cover.

Shrapnel shot into the fish soup. Katya turned away, but not fast enough. Fish landed on her shoulders, sat on her head, and hung from her nurse's veil.

When the shelling stopped, Katya climbed down from the platform and walked sedately toward her own wheeled soup kitchen. She pretended not to hear the guffaws all around her.

Later, during a solemn ceremony held for soldiers receiving decorations, Katya started when the General's assistant called out from the make-shift stage, "Nurse Ekaterina de Hueck, please step forward."

Puzzled, she did as instructed.

"For bravery under fire," the assistant read aloud, "you are awarded the Medal of the Order of St. Anne."

A few isolated chuckles among the soldiers fanned into widespread laughter.

"What is the meaning of this breach of military etiquette?" the General demanded, pinning on Katya's medal.

Trying to keep a straight face, Katya stepped back to join the line of other award-winning soldiers.

On the ground, an officer stepped forward and said, "General, truly Nurse de Hueck exhibited great bravery, but . . ." and he told the story.

The General smiled, kissed Katya on both cheeks, and dismissed her.

Not long after that, Katya picked up yet another assignment, to act as hostess in the Welcome Tent. She organized games, visited with the newcomers, and joined the soldiers and nurses in singing their beloved Russian folk songs and ballads. She kept the atmosphere light, but always dreaded the next morning, when the strong, healthy young men went out to fight. In a few hours or days, these soldiers would be dead, or have an arm or leg missing. By day, Katya spent long hours helping to patch up the wounded soldiers she visited with in the evening. What made it doubly hard to take was knowing that many of the casualties were caused by the absence of proper equipment. Russia lacked the financial stability of the German army. Thousands of uniformed Russian peasants didn't have guns until the soldiers in front of them got killed or wounded, and their weapons made available.

Katya heard that in an attempt to raise morale, the government changed the name of the capital to Petrograd, Russianizing the original German name. The change didn't appear to do much good. In the city of the new name, leaders of the rebellious Bolshevik Revolutionary Party called the war a rich man's battle, and urged workers to stop toiling at the mills, loading docks, and factories. Under this same Bolshevik influence, peasants started refusing to work the land. Mechanics stayed home; and trains stopped bringing food to the troops. Men Katya had never seen before at the Front cried out,

"Go home, soldiers! Kill the landowners! Seize their land, and grow all the food you want for yourselves!"

The troops stirred; and Katya trembled. These radical new Bolsheviks meant big trouble.

Food supplies dwindled to only a few days' backup. Katya's superior sent her and a cavalcade of at least twenty drays and their drivers to a camp over forty miles away. Slowed down by hunger and fatigue on the part of both men and animals, the trip took almost two full days.

When they finally reached their destination, the camp's Lieutenant said he had his own trouble. A mile away, his men were trapped by the Germans on a spit of land surrounded on three sides by a wide river. They had been there over three days, without ammunition or food. The Lieutenant had tried sending supplies by rail, but the Germans stopped them every time.

Using the Lieutenant's field glasses, Katya saw a single railroad track leading to the finger of land. She also saw overturned freight cars on the sides of the track, and the bodies of many dead soldiers among the demolished hunks of steel. Sick at heart, but thinking fast, Katya got an idea.

"The German guns must be set high enough for freight cars and engines," she said. "The shells should go right over a horse-drawn flatcar. We could do it."

The Lieutenant hesitated, and shrugged. "Nothing else has worked. Try it."

Katya and ten of her drivers lay in the middle of a flatcar, surrounded by bags of flour, straw, and other supplies. She urged the two horses pulling the car into a gallop. German shells whined over the flatcar, not finding their range until too late.

Her mission accomplished, Katya led her drivers at a crawl back to the Lieutenant under the cover of darkness and the protective fire of the newly-armed Russian soldiers. Within moments of their return to the Lieutenant, Katya and her men loaded up the sought-after emergency supplies, and brought them back to their own camp. For her part in the daring escapade, Katya received a recommendation for the Cross of St. George, Russia's highest military honor for bravery under fire. She could hardly wait to receive it and take it home to show her father.

Katya in her nurse's uniform, World War I

Chapter 6

A New Threat

"It was only too plain that mob mentality was beginning to assert itself and that not only the beast but the fool in man was striving to gain the upper hand."

(Pitirim Sorokin: *A Long Journey*)

In the Red Cross tent behind the front lines, Katya treated the wounds of an engineering officer named Nicholas Makletzoff. His wife had died three years before, and his small daughter lived with her grandmother. Katya, now almost twenty and starved for affection, warmed under the lamp of tenderness that Nicholas shone on her. She knew that as a married woman, she couldn't pursue the possibility of a serious relationship, but she couldn't bear to push Nicholas away, either. She prayed to know what to do.

Before she could get a full grasp of her mixed-up emotions, Katya received a middle of the night plea for nursing help in the forest, where fighting had broken out. She saddled her horse, and rode across the field toward the woods. Still half asleep, she drifted off in the saddle as her horse cantered down the dirt path. The next thing Katya knew, the horse had jumped over a narrow stream at the edge of the forest, and she was slipping from his back. As she fell, her nurse's cape fluttered in the breeze, frightening the horse. Before Katya could roll aside, the skittish animal reared, kicking her in the back.

Tsar Nicholas II and his family, all executed in July, 1918, by the Bolsheviks

When Katya regained consciousness, she felt the horse's tongue licking her face. Remembering her mission, she tried to lift herself back into the saddle. Pain shot through her back and side. She coughed, and realized she was spitting up blood. Clenching her jaw, she shut her mind to everything but the need to reach the wounded troops. She got her foot into the stirrup, and somehow swung herself into the saddle.

Katya urged the horse into a gallop, and soon reached the trenches. There was no medical help present at all. Forgetting about her injury, Katya set to work nursing the wounded. Sometime past dawn, a doctor arrived. He took one look at the wounded, one look at Katya, and told her to go to the base hospital. He thought she might have a torn lung from the horse's kick.

Soon ordered on sick leave, Katya packed her scant belongings for the train trip to Petrograd. She took along a new word in her vocabulary: communism. The radical Bolsheviks claimed to have what the country needed—new rulers who worked for the common good of all Russians. Katya feared the Bolshevik claims. She had already seen the damage they had caused in the war effort.

As Katya headed toward home, Tsar Nicholas II assumed what he believed to be his absolute responsibility as the high commander of the army. His military inexperience jeopardized both the war effort and the fraying thread of confidence left in the Tsarist Regime. Grigori Rasputin, a self-proclaimed healer-monk who had wormed his way into the inner circle of the

Grigori Rasputin, assassinated in December, 1916

Tsar and his family, had already weakened the people's confidence in their leader. Rasputin claimed he could cure Tsar Nicholas's young son Alexis of hemophilia; but most Russians feared the intruder's real intention of being at court was to discover military secrets for the German army. Plots to assassinate Rasputin broke out among several political groups.

Vladimir Lenin, founding leader of the Bolshevik Party, utilized the aura of uncertainty to cause more civil unrest and confusion. By the time Katya reached Petrograd, she learned that Bolshevik-incited strikes, riots, and chaos plagued the whole country.

While Katya was still in Petrograd on sick leave, a group of disaffected aristocrats murdered Rasputin. Most Russians reacted with relief; but his death came too late. Confidence in the monarchy had lost too much ground.

Katya, too, had lost ground. Sick, and struggling to stay alive in a city almost without food, she couldn't imagine life getting any more uncertain—until Nicholas Makletzoff showed up on her doorstep.

Chapter 7

Subversive Activity

"If Justice travels for ten years, she will never find shelter in the castles of the powerful."

(Russian proverb)

Nicholas's presence threw Katya into turmoil. Like a ball player caught off base, she flipped back and forth between ecstasy and despair. It got more complicated when her father met Nicholas and discovered he had nowhere to go for the Christmas holidays. Fyodor invited him to go with the family to Antrea, Finland. Tambov was too far away from St. Petersburg for short vacations; so the past several years the Kolyschkines had been going to Emma's ancestral estate, only a hundred miles away.

In Antrea, pulled toward Nicholas, but straining to stay faithful to her marriage vows, Katya finally reached a painful decision. She asked Nicholas to leave. Heartsick, she, too, soon left Antrea.

She returned to Petrograd, where regiments of soldiers refused to disperse gathering street mobs. The stench of decaying garbage strewn all over the sidewalks filled the air. Bolshevik-led gangs ripped apart the city's bridges. Special police forces shot into the crowds, killing many and inciting further rage. Cannons and machine guns appeared on rooftops and in high windows. Police stations and other buildings symbolizing authority were set on fire, with the flames spreading to private dwellings. The Tsarist government shuffled to regain control.

Katya wedged through the crowds toward her flat on Geslerovsky Street. Near home, she stopped short at the sight of a tall, too-thin soldier walking toward her. What was Boris doing home? Her mind raced. When she had left on sick leave, she had also left Boris. Was she ready to return to him? It would be the gospel thing to do, the loving and forgiving thing to do. She straightened her shoulders, took a deep breath, and called out to him.

Boris had been granted a leave to attend the funeral of his stepfather, and to gain strength. Katya accompanied him home, and found out that the Bolsheviks had seized control of the banks. No aristocrats had access to their own money. No money meant no food and no fuel for heating their apartment.

Determined not to give up and die, Katya spent the next several days bartering their cutlery, dishes, and clothing for food. When the apartment lay bare except for the furniture they needed to chop up for fuel, Katya put on her old snow-shoveling coat and began "shopping". Under the cover of early evening twilight, she clawed through the garbage cans of the Bolsheviks, the only people in Petrograd who had leftovers.

One evening, as Katya walked down a littered side street, a gang of drunken Bolsheviks swaggered toward her.

"A bourgeois!" one spluttered.

The men lurched at Katya, pushing her against a stucco building where a torn theater poster flapped against the bullet-ridden wall. One man fired his pistol. Katya flung her hand in front of her face. Pain shattered her awareness, and she slid down the wall to the sidewalk.

By the time she revived, the Bolsheviks had gone. She tried to wipe the blood from her face, but her hand didn't work right. It dawned on her that her head was unhurt, but her hand was a mess. She struggled to her feet, and made her way home to bandage it as well as she could.

The Russian social structure kept unraveling; and Katya's father began moving books, furniture, carpets, and family heirlooms across the border to Finland. Convinced, though, that political stability would soon be restored, he stayed in Petrograd to work. Katya's thirteen-year-old brother Serge stayed with him, to complete his school year.

Not yet well enough to return to the Front with Boris, Katya went back to Antrea to help her mother organize the family possessions Fyodor had sent. Trading and bartering food and goods with neighbors and friends kept them all alive; and the approach of spring promised hope in the form of a new growing season.

In March, 1917, while Katya was in Antrea, Tsar Nicholas II abdicated the throne for himself and his son Alexis. Nicholas's brother, Grand Duke Michael, refused to step in; and a Provisional Government, headed by Alexander Kerensky, took over the reins of leadership. Lenin and the Bolsheviks demanded an end to Russia's part in the war and the transfer of all power to the Soviets. The Provisional Government wavered; and, in short order, Bolshevism and anarchy prevailed.

In the midst of all the uncertainty, Katya returned to the Front, where many soldiers, heeding the Bolshevik propaganda, turned against the authority of their commanders. In her role as Red Cross nurse's aide, Katya began slipping medical passes to officers in danger of being assassinated by their own men. Disguised as wounded soldiers, they disappeared from the battlefield to safety. Katya knew that the possibility of getting caught for her part in the deception grew with every false pass she signed.

Katya's mother's family estate in Antrea, Finland

Bolshevik soldiers in St. Petersburg during the Russian Revolution

Chapter 8

Bolshevik Encounter

"The abyss has opened at last. Bolshevism has conquered."

(Pitirim Sorokin: *A Long Journey*)

Katya could almost feel rough strands of rope tighten around her neck when, in the fall of 1917, Bolshevik soldiers took over the camp. It came almost as a relief when an orderly appeared and escorted her to the new company commander.

Nerves taut, Katya stepped into a dingy little room in a cabin near the hospital. The Bolshevik soldier in charge lolled in a tipped back wooden chair, his feet propped up on the desk. When Katya appeared, he scrambled to his feet, waved the orderly away, and bowed low before her.

Katya's eyes widened.

"I sent for you, Nurse," the soldier said, "because of a certain incident."

Katya started at the man's lisp, and saw that he had a missing front tooth.

"Yes," she said, trying to keep her voice from quivering. "I remember."

The soldier flashed a brief smile.

"I would never have forgiven myself if I had been allowed to follow through with my intention. I owe you a favor."

"Thank you." Where was this conversation going, Katya wondered.

The soldier sat down again, resting his forearms on the desk. "We have discovered," he said, "that someone is signing false Red Cross passes for officers. The nurse who's doing it is in grave danger."

Katya's fingers closed around the warm steel of the Derringer hidden in the sleeve of her nurse's uniform. She hoped her face didn't betray her alarm.

"There is a saddled horse at the edge of the woods." The soldier talked fast now. "Ride north. A woman living in the farmhouse at the crossroads will give you peasant clothing."

By the next morning, after a fitful sleep in the peasant's barn, Katya trudged along the dirt road toward Petrograd. She wished she could have kept the horse, but people were being shot for a lot less than owning a horse. She wondered as she walked how Boris would take her sudden disappearance. Worn down from his abuse, she had moved out of their cabin, and hardly saw him anymore; but he would notice her total absence from the unit. She prayed for his safety from the Germans and from his men.

Dust billowed up from the road, burning her injured lung. She coughed, and coughed again.

Along the way, more and more travelers clogged the road: hungry army deserters, ill-clad farm workers, and angry peasants in search of scraps of food for their crying children. At night, Katya huddled among them for warmth, and tried to sleep. By day, she shuffled along against the wind. When at last she spotted the golden dome of St. Isaac's Cathedral shimmering in the dust, she fell to her knees and cried. Not for long. Crying took energy, and she needed all she had to reach her father and home.

After two days and several long coughing spells, Katya's father sent her to a doctor. He confirmed that Katya had tuberculosis. Hearing the verdict, Katya longed for Nicholas and his gentle, consoling presence. She wrote in her diary,

"They told me I was sick with tuberculosis. This doesn't make any difference. Tried to write to Nicholas. Kolya, Kolya. Where is he? What is he doing? Why is each thought of him a little piece of happiness for me?"

Instead of Nicholas, Boris appeared. He had hidden in the basement of the officers' cabin in order to escape execution by his men. He, too, suffered from hunger and sickness.

Katya left her father and brother and took up her old routine of scrounging for food in the garbage cans of the Bolsheviks.

On October 25, 1917, the Bolsheviks seized total power in Petrograd. The Provisional Government collapsed. As Katya listened from her apartment, she shivered with fear at the sounds of rifle fire and cannon ball explosions. When the gunfire ceased, an eerie stillness settled over the city.

"No sound of streetcars or of any other traffic disturbed the deathlike silence," Katya wrote. "It was as if the city had died or was crouching there like a stalked beast, afraid to breathe."

Katya and Boris left Petrograd, and went to Antrea. Boris got a job in nearby Vyborg and sometimes stayed there overnight. On one such night, Katya wrote,

"It is very sad. It is night. The wind is howling. I am not sleeping. God be praised, Boris is not here. Beginning with the moment I came back to him, my joy and tranquility are gone." Still, she decided to stay in Antrea for the time being. Her father and Serge came for the Christmas holidays.

On January 1, 1918, twenty-one-year-old Katya received a diary from her twenty-eight-year-old husband. On the flyleaf, he inscribed, in verse,

"Here you must write down everything that happens to you in the course of the day, and remember also that what's mine is always dear to me. And so you must keep every line at any given time open to my perusal. I hope in this little book during this new year I'll not come across any offensive deed, much less a nasty thought.

"Your, Boris"

Under this poetically couched warning, Katya began the New Year. All of Russia, too, began the year on an ominous note. As war and revolution tore away at the country's weakening fabric, Katya got ready to return to the Front. The commanding officers of her company were now being elected by their men. The rotation of officers meant that Katya would not be recognized. Boris would be working with a new regiment of soldiers. It would be all right.

Leaving Antrea, Katya and Boris first went to their *dacha* near Kiskile, Finland. Boris had built *Merri-Lokki*, the Sea Gull, on a rocky ledge by the sea. Katya was sorry she and Boris could only spend a few days there before continuing on their journey to the Front.

Once at their unit, Boris found out he was due for a furlough, followed by his discharge from the army. Katya felt like dancing, and doubly so when Colonel Bastrakov, the unit commander, awarded her the promised Medal of St. George.

When Katya left the Front and arrived in the desolate wasteland of a ravished Petrograd, her joy vanished. She agreed with Boris that they had to try and get back to *Merri-Lokki*. The Red Guard would never let two aristocrats cross into Finland, so they traveled on foot by night, through knee-deep snow.

Many scattered pockets of Christians kept the faith alive in the face of growing persecution by the Bolsheviks.

"A Secluded Monastery" by Vitali Linitsky

Basilica of St. Basil, Moscow, by Bichebois

Chapter 9

Caught!

"Out of the depths I cry to You, O Lord."
(Psalm 130)

𝒩ear the border, Katya and Boris hid in a peasant's pigsty until, one moonless night Katya took Boris's arm and crept with him to the gully that divided Russia from Finland. She slid down the steep bank into the ravine, and crawled on sharp rocks through the icy water of a shallow, fast-moving stream.

Finnish Guards heard the scuffling, and opened fire.

"Don't shoot!" Katya cried out in Finnish.

Her command of the language got her and Boris out of danger, into a friendly rapport with the Finnish police, and onto a train bound for Kiskile.

Katya reveled in the ordinary days of country life at *Merri-Lokki*; but she spent fretful, sleepless nights. Nobody had heard from her father and brother in Petrograd. Unable to stand the ominous silence, she and Boris snuck across the border to look for them. After three days of frantic searching, they had to return to Kiskile without a trace of either of them.

On March 3, 1918, the Bolsheviks signed the Treaty of Brest-Litovsk, agreeing to a separate peace with the invading Germans. It was the only way Lenin could be sure his new Soviet state would survive. The vast majority of Russians believed the country should continue to support the allied cause; and the treaty triggered an all-out Russian civil war.

Inside Katya and Boris's dacha, Merri-Lokki, near Kiskile, Finland

As Katya cleaned, cooked, and prepared land for a vegetable garden at *Merri-Lokki*, the Bolsheviks, now officially the Communists, set out from their new government headquarters in Moscow to crush all opposition. The Tcheka (Secret Police) arrested and executed any and all suspected anti-Communists.

A lot of Finnish citizens didn't know yet that, as a result of the Brest-Litovsk Treaty, their country had received its freedom from Russian rule. In border towns like Kiskile, Finland's Red Guard still recruited many young men.

Katya kept her sanity through it all by hard physical work, study and reading. Her old desire to become closer to God grew strong again. She wrote in her diary,

"Lord, let me take Your cross and walk in Your footsteps, even though I'm not worthy."

To sustain life, she and Boris fished for smelt in the nearby sea. They ate some of the fish and used the rest to barter for other food. In late spring, the garden produced new vegetable shoots; and Katya breathed a sigh of relief. Except for the terrible fear for her father and brother, things were looking up.

Finnish Red Guards shattered any illusion of well-being when they appeared at the *dacha* and arrested Boris. As Katya stood helpless in the doorway, the Guards hauled Boris away.

Dacha and outer buildings of Merri-Lokki

Nightmarish days and nights followed, until one afternoon, without explanation, the Guards brought Boris back home. Overjoyed, Katya went out for a celebratory walk with him in the forest. As they returned to *Merri-Lokki*, Katya spotted some of the local villagers walking up the hill toward them.

"Isn't that nice," she thought. "They're coming to see if Boris is all right." And then she saw the red bands on their arms.

Katya grabbed Boris's hand; and they turned to run. Before they could get more than a few yards, they were surrounded by villagers, many of them neighbors and friends.

In a mock trial outside *Merri-Lokki*, the Guards decided Katya and Boris were enemies of the people and should die by slow starvation in their own *dacha*. The Guards removed what little food they found in the cabin, but left wood for heat and water to drink, so as to prolong their suffering.

In the agonizing days of hunger that followed, Katya fell in and out of consciousness. As if in a dream, she saw a guard let a dog with a bone loose in the *dacha*. Boris saw it too. They half-ran, half-crawled to the dog. Boris snatched the bone from the snarling dog. Katya clawed at Boris to wrench the bone from his grasp. He slapped her away. The bone fell to the floor, and they and the dog dove for it. Suddenly, with an anguished cry, Katya and Boris looked at each other. What were they doing! Boris handed Katya the bone. She gnawed on it, and handed it back. When they had licked and chewed the almost meatless bone to a bare shine, Boris tossed it out the door. The dog trotted after it.

During periods of ensuing lucidity, Katya came to realize that, because of her former privileged lifestyle, she was, in part, responsible for the grief that now tore her country to pieces. Sorrow overtook her, until, in the heart of her pain, she felt encompassed by the peace and forgiveness of Christ. A longing rose in her to share this peace with others, even though, for her, it was probably too late.

While Katya lay starving to death, the German army moved to prevent Russia from taking back Finland's independence. When German soldiers poured into the border towns to wipe out all the remaining Communist pockets, a small patrol arrived in Kiskile and arrested most of the villagers. These same soldiers discovered

Katya and Boris, and transported them to the hospital in Vyborg, near Antrea.

At first, hallucinations fogged Katya's mind, and she could only take an occasional tablespoon of water. In time, though, her mind cleared, and her body began to accept food. Soon, the doctor pronounced her well, and added that she was a miracle. The starvation should have made her tuberculosis worse, but, although she had the scars of it, she was cured.

Some weeks after they had been brought into the hospital on stretchers, Katya and Boris left on their own wobbly feet. At eighty-five pounds, Katya looked like a skeleton with flesh draped over it. Not wanting to take her mother by surprise, she knocked on the door at Antrea.

Emma opened the door. "Yes, Madam, what can I do for . . . Aiee! Katya! My Katyushka!" she cried, and fainted at Katya's feet.

Chapter 10

Hard-Won Foundations

*"Here, and nowhere else, is where the effective
defense of peace must begin—with the defense of
spiritual values in the soul of every human being."*

(Alexander Solzhenitsyn: *The Oak and the Calf*)

*W*hen Fyodor and Serge materialized in a refugee
camp outside Vyborg, freedom from worry about
them helped speed up Katya's recovery. They, too, came
to Antrea to recuperate from hunger and the constant
dodging of the Tcheka. Their last secret residence had
been the hull of Guido de Hueck's boat, docked at the
Petersburg Yacht Club.

Boris's father, who had brought his wife Martha and
their two young sons to live in Finland, called to invite
Fyodor to breakfast. Fyodor accepted; and, to Katya's
relief, this put an end to the long feud between her father
and Boris's.

The hostilities in her homeland didn't fare as well. In July, 1918, the Bolsheviks murdered the entire royal family and hundreds of anti-Bolshevik revolutionaries.

Temporarily distanced from the traumas of war and revolution, Katya had time to take stock of how she wanted to live her life. She realized she, like the pilgrims she had known as a child, longed to live by the Russian ideals symbolized by the holy city of Grad Kitezh.

Built in the twelfth century, Grad Kitezh was founded and ruled by the Gospel principles of peace, love, and selfless service. The existence of such a place in their midst provided a source of hope for the oppressed, war-torn people of early Rus.

Grad Kitezh sinking into the Svetloyar (Ashmolean Museum, University of Oxford)

History records that in the thirteenth century, Grad Kitezh was attacked, every building destroyed, and every inhabitant massacred by Batu Khan and his "Golden Horde" of Mongolian warriors. Devastated by the loss of the city and its ideals, the people of Rus gradually regained their hope by developing a legend that claimed victory in the terrible loss. The legend claims that God sank Grad Kitezh into the nearby Svetloyar, the Beautiful Lake, thus preserving forever the city and its faithful Christian citizens. Throughout the following centuries, the so often downtrodden Russian people, who longed for a better way of life, searched for the hidden city of selfless love and peace.

In order to begin her own journey to Gospel peace, Katya felt she had to face the drawbacks in her character that blocked her intentions. She discovered these were not so different from her faults as a child.

"I'm trying to be a better person," she wrote in August, 1918. "Don't know if I can manage it."

While she was trying to get her own life in order, Katya picked up another challenge. She was barely twenty-two, but in the burgeoning Russian refugee camp developing around Antrea, the others looked to her for consolation and leadership. Trying to meet their expectations, Katya searched the Gospels for strength, hope, and a love that would bring peace to the taut nerves of squabbling refugees.

Yet another challenge threw Katya into turmoil. Boris developed a roving eye, and more than a casual interest in other women. At first, Katya pored over the Gospels, searching for a way to meet this new trial with peace, love, and forgiveness. But, finally, she cracked. Driven by pain, confusion, and rage, she flung aside her attempts at becoming a better person. She abandoned her diet, told wild exaggerations, gossiped, and soaked up the praise that people heaped on her for her tutoring efforts with the children of the Russian refugee families.

For a moment, a glance at a newspaper pulled her thoughts away from her personal struggles to a broader field. World War I ended on November 11, 1918, with the signing of the Armistice outside Paris; but the news from Russia was horrific. The "Red Terror" was in full swing, with Lenin and the Bolsheviks hunting down and murdering countless suspected anti-Communists. In the refugee camp, everyone's nerves frayed to the breaking point.

Poverty, too, tore at Katya's spirits the way her thinning clothes tore at the seams. Inactivity made her crave action. Boris's coldness toward her made her life tedious, and then tragic. An unrecorded incident that involved him devastated her.

"It is the month of May," she wrote in her diary in 1919. "I am so exhausted. . . . I am a stupid, stupid woman. I am out of my mind. Why did all this happen? Why? O God! They say that everything You do is for the best. Can this be for the best? It cannot be! . . . Boris, my one and only, my beloved. Today I was so angry again. I feel awful. What will become of this?"

Chapter 11

Murmansk

*"In great pain, the tears flow from the heart,
not from the eye."*

(Russian Proverb)

*B*efore Katya could recover from whatever happened with Boris, she was thrown together with him in a new, hazardous adventure. The White Army needed recruits. World War I was over, but some of the Allied countries, afraid that the Bolsheviks meant to spread their power all over Europe, kept soldiers on the Russian Civil War battlefield to help fight Communism.

At the White Army headquarters in Helsingfors (now Helsinki), Finland, Boris received a new commission as Major. Katya signed on as a nurse's aide with the British Red Cross, serving with the Syren Force of Britain's North Russian Expeditionary Force. They were sent to the northernmost Russian seaport of Murmansk, one hundred and fifty miles above the Artic Circle. Formerly a tiny fishing village, Murmansk now served as an

Allied post under British command. Boris helped with the ongoing construction of the wilderness base. Katya worked at a field hospital about ten miles outside the village.

One evening, in the middle of her rounds at the field hospital, she got a call to come into town and do some translating. Katya went to the little railroad depot hidden in the hills to wait for the train that would take her back to headquarters.

Inside the station, she eyed a large pile of loose hay stored in the corner for the hospital staff's horses. Worn out, cold and sleepy, and with an hour's wait ahead of her, Katya snuggled into the hay for a nap. She awoke at the sound of men's voices speaking in Finnish, bragging about how they were "going to use the dynamite." Katya caught her breath. For the past week, there had been panicked talk at headquarters about the theft of a consignment of dynamite.

The train rumbled into the station yard; and Katya heard booted feet leaving the depot. When she was as sure as possible that the men wouldn't see her through a window, she slipped out of the hay pile and went out to the station platform. Three men were climbing into the first of two train cars. For a moment, Katya held back, and then entered the second car. When the train chugged into motion, she brushed the last straws of hay from her nurse's uniform, willed her racing heart to slow down, and ambled into the first car. She found a seat near the men.

Unaware that Katya understood Finnish, the Communists finished working out their plan to blow up the Murmansk outpost. Katya hid her excitement as she got off the train at headquarters. When the British officers asked her to translate some Russian letters dealing

Katya and Boris on way to Murmansk

Katya (top middle) and Boris
(bottom middle) with group in
Murmansk

Nurses' quarters in Murmansk

Katya (wearing her St. George's medal for
bravery) and two British doctors, Murmansk

Solovetsky Monastery in the White Sea

A "typical Russian monk"

The last train out of Murmansk

Refugees sleeping in a boat outside Murmansk

with the stolen explosives, she announced that she knew where they were.

Relishing her moment of triumph, Katya told the gathered officers what she had heard. As a result, the thieves were arrested, the dynamite was repossessed, and Katya was awarded a decoration by the British government.

A month or so later, Katya and Boris received a short military leave. Together, they went on a pilgrimage to the White Sea islands of Solovetsky. The Solovetsky Monastery, founded in 1429, had been an ongoing place of pilgrimage for thousands of Russians. Katya and Boris wanted to get a blessing from the holy monks there.

They had come at a wonderful time, the Abbot said. That very day, he had recalled a *staretz*, a holy elder, from his *poustinia*, his wilderness cell, where he had lived and prayed for thirty years. Katya and Boris, the Abbot said, could visit him.

They entered a simple, almost bare room. A frail old man with silver hair that made a halo around his head sat on a rough-hewn bench. His straggly gray beard stretched low over his chest. His pink cheeks, though lined, glowed with health. He looked at Katya through the clear blue eyes of a child.

Following a short visit, the *staretz* blessed Boris with stern words of reprimand, referring to him as a bad apple spoiling the others around him.

When the monk placed his hand on Katya's head, she felt her heart leap with joy.

"Katya, beloved of Mary," the *staretz* said. "Your sign is the cross. Don't fight it. For He who is crucified on it waits for you and loves you. Your breasts will feed Him who is thirsty; and from your womb His children shall spring up, if you are faithful. Be faithful, child of sorrow, whose eyes shall see the eyes of God."

The monk lifted Katya's chin, looked into her eyes, and said,

"Child, you are predestined by God to do great works for Him. You will suffer much and know Christ's pain; but don't be afraid. You will also know His joy. Follow where He leads. Go in His footsteps."

The old monk's words burned into Katya's heart, until she and Boris got back to Murmansk, and she found out the British were planning to evacuate. They said it didn't look as though the Bolsheviks' power was going to spread any farther than Russia; and the British soldiers had had it with war. They wanted to go home. Their leaving would put any White Russian left in Murmansk at great risk.

Boris had developed pleurisy and other lung trouble, and both the British base commander and the medical staff said he should leave the country at once. They could get him on the last medical ship. Katya could get on as his nurse.

Katya felt sick at the thought of leaving Russia without seeing her family or getting word to them; but she realized the urgency of evacuating. There wouldn't be another chance. She accepted a place with Boris on the international ship bound for a military hospital in Edinburgh, Scotland.

Dunya Vassova, a young native of Murmansk who had been employed at the nurses' station, begged to go along. There was nothing for her in Murmansk, she told Katya, besides death at the hands of the Bolsheviks.

Unaware of it at the time, Katya made a decision that proved to be as much a blessing for her as it was for Dunya. She accepted the girl as a companion; and in September, 1919, Katya, Boris, and Dunya left Russia and sailed to the other side of the world.

Chapter 12

By Paths Unknown

"By paths unknown, I will guide them."
(Isaiah 42: 16)

Katya sewing in London, 1919-1921

*W*hen Boris got well enough to leave the hospital in Edinburgh, the British army offered to send him and Katya, travel expenses paid, to anywhere in the Commonwealth. They chose London, England, where Katya found lodging in a barren attic room of the YMCA. She tucked Boris into bed, and went out to find a bank. A teller informed her that Russian currency had dropped so low on the world market that her entire savings of 10,000 rubles was worth only a few English pounds.

In a panic, Katya took to the streets, looking for work. Thanks to her experience in Murmansk, she landed a job with the British Red Cross, sewing underwear for soldiers. What she earned barely kept her and Boris alive. She prayed for two miracles—a better job and to have a child.

Boris at his desk

Boris reminded her of the scarcity of jobs in London and that her TB and starvation made it impossible for her to have a baby.

Feeling robbed of her last strands of hope, Katya took to going for long walks after work. One evening, she came across a convent in Bayswater that belonged to the Sisters of Sion. Waves of happy memories from her schooldays in Egypt washed over her. She walked up the stone steps and rang the convent bell.

From that time on, Katya went often to visit the Sisters. In their presence, she regained her peace and experienced a renewed desire to serve the poor like St. Francis of Assisi had. There were plenty of opportunities. From Constantinople to Shanghai, Russian refugees faced poverty, despair, hopelessness, and the tearing apart of families. Katya had little herself, but she shared what she had with

Katya, reading

the other refugees in London. Sometimes, all she had to give was a word of sympathy.

Propelled by her re-kindled faith, Katya decided to become a Roman Catholic. Her Russian Orthodox friends called her a traitor. Their hostility hurt. Katya felt sure she was doing what God wanted her to do; but she loved her Orthodox heritage too. From the time she made her formal entry into the Roman Catholic Church, she worked toward unity between Eastern and Western Christian spirituality.

One thing Katya's renewed faith and purpose in life couldn't do was find her a better job. Boris felt there was only one solution to their desperate financial situation. They had to go to the Russian Embassy and sign up for service in the southern Russian White Army, which still fought the Bolsheviks. Katya recoiled at the thought, but she couldn't come up with any other plan.

At the Embassy, the tall, elegantly dressed Undersecretary behind the desk spotted the family crest on Boris's ring, and leaped from his chair.

"A de Hueck!" he cried. "I am Walter de Hueck, from Estonia!"

By the time Katya and Boris left the office, they had an invitation to live with Uncle Walter and his wife Ebba in the upscale West End of London. Boris had a job at the Embassy as Technical Advisor to the Financial Attaché; and as soon as Katya mastered shorthand, she got a job as a stenographer.

With their steady incomes, Katya and Boris were able to move from Uncle Walter's to a place of their own in Notting Hill. Dunya Vassova, who had been working for an English officer, left him and came to be with Katya as a live-in maid. At last, Katya thought, we can begin to live normal lives. If it weren't for worrying about her family and friends in Finland, she felt she would almost be happy.

Katya's good fortune didn't last. In another quick turn of events, the Bolsheviks took total control in Russia. The Embassy in London closed. Uncle Walter and Aunt Ebba moved back home to Estonia. Katya and Boris moved into increasingly smaller flats in London. Boris couldn't find work; but eventually, Katya got another job as a stenographer. The pay was barely enough to keep her, Boris, and Dunya alive. Still, Dunya insisted on staying and helping them, working for no more than a roof over her head and a bite to eat.

Katya and Dunya

Katya came up with an idea. Why not start a laundry? She and Dunya got it going. The added work helped stave off their downhill financial spiral; but it didn't stop Boris from returning to his abusive ways and tormenting Katya. It didn't stop the bouts of nausea Katya started experiencing, either. Not knowing what else to do, she went to the doctor.

"You're expecting," he told her.

His words sent Katya into ecstasy. Her life with Boris remained dark, but inside, her heart glowed with light. Throughout the fall of 1920, she clung to the joy of expecting a child.

When she fell down a department store flight of stairs on a Christmas shopping expedition, the doctor put her on strict bed rest for the duration of her pregnancy. Boris's behavior improved; and Katya and he spent a quiet but happy Christmas.

At the beginning of 1921, widespread famine broke out in Russia. In London, bedridden Katya, along with friends who could do the leg work, raised funds for their suffering countrymen. In the United States, Secretary of Commerce, Herbert Hoover, organized massive food drives.

Katya's mother Emma in Antrea

In the midst of the crisis, H. B. Dunnington-Grubb, a landscape architect from Toronto, Canada, offered Boris a job as a draftsman. It hurt Katya to think of going even farther away from all those she loved in Russia and Finland. The one consolation she found in moving was that Ontario sounded like Russia in its climate and vast forests.

Katya breathed easier, too, when the Dunnington-Grubbs said they would pay the fare for Dunya as well as for Katya and Boris. Not only had Dunya demonstrated her love and service in so many ways already, but Katya would need her even more as she prepared to have a baby in a new and strange land.

Katya on board ship, going to Canada

On March 19, 1921, Katya rode on a stretcher to the steamship S. S. Minnedosa, ready to set sail on another unknown path.

Chapter 13

Refugee Mother

*"Possessions bring worries;
poverty has them already."*

(Russian Proverb)

Katya expecting, in Toronto, April 1921

Flash bulbs popped as Katya was being carried off the ship on the eastern shore of Canada. People with notebooks and pens shot questions at her about the Russian Revolution and her expected child. The words "Baron" and "Baroness" flew around her like verbal confetti. From her prone position on the stretcher, Katya looked up at Boris.

"I heard that Americans like titles," he murmured in Russian; "so on the passenger list I registered us as Baron and Baroness de Hueck."

Katya shook her head. They had never used their titles before. Too ostentatious.

Katya and baby George, July 1921

Soon after arriving in Toronto, Katya contacted Archbishop Neil McNeil. In Holy Russia, the local bishop was the father of one's soul. It gave Katya comfort to tap into the spiritual roots of her new home. Now, she was ready.

On July 17, 1921, Katya gave birth to George Theodore Mario de Hueck. She didn't think it possible to be any happier.

Her peak moment descended into anxiety when Boris lost or quit his job at the Dunnington-Grubb plant nursery. Dunya couldn't legally work for pay until the following summer. So, Katya had to place her baby in Dunya's care, and go to work at menial jobs. Her salary barely kept them afloat.

Finally Boris found a job as a carpet designer and architect. His

George as a toddler

added income saved their new little home on Nairn Avenue; but then he began spending more money than he made. Katya had to keep everyone fed on the produce she grew in her backyard garden. Instead of wanting to become poor like St. Francis now, she only wanted to get out from the terrible strain of destitution.

In the spring of 1923, Katya's father died. Serge, who had come to Toronto to study medicine, returned to Finland. Then he, Andrew, and their mother moved to Belgium, where they scratched out a meager living.

Katya sent whatever she could to help them. At the same time, she did her best to help the new wave of refugees in Toronto. When Claudia Kolenova landed at the train station with nowhere to go, Katya took her into her own home.

Boris

During the first months of 1924, at the request of the other refugees, Katya spearheaded the building of a Russian Orthodox Church, and organized a charity bazaar to raise money for a Russian Community Center. The city newspapers called the event "a smashing success", but Boris "borrowed" seventy-five dollars from the proceeds. When Katya found out, she panicked. She had no idea how to pay back such a large sum.

Claudia Kolenova

Soon after the bazaar, Katya discovered that Boris was having an affair with Claudia. Humiliated and grieved, Katya had to work hard at being a cheerful sales clerk at T.

Eaton's downtown store. She managed it though, and people seemed to enjoy chatting with her. One woman, Marietta La Dell, wrote Katya a letter, inviting her to join the Canadian Community Chautauqua, an organization that provided high-quality entertainment and education to small rural communities that had no other way of being in touch with culture, music, drama, and intellectual presentations.

"It will be the small but *excellent* beginning of *great* things for you," Miss La Dell wrote. "I have great faith in your ability & message [of combating Communism with Christian love and service]. Chautauqua will certainly be a stepping-stone lined with gold. This is a prophecy that I expect to come true!! You are young, good to look at, of rare intelligence and have 'food for thought.'"

With a flicker of hope, Katya accepted Miss La Dell's offer for the fall Chautauqua circuit. Meanwhile, she needed money for her family and other struggling refugees a lot sooner than that. She turned to her parish priest, Fr. Edward McCabe, for advice. He suggested she go to New York, get a better-paying job, and bring Boris and George there. That would get Boris away from Claudia's grip. Meanwhile, Dunya could look after George.

Katya and George

Katya walked away from the church carrying a mixture of fear, anxiety, hope, renewed determination, and the train fare to New York.

Chapter 14

The City of Many Faces

"Hope is more a food of the poor than of the rich."
(Russian Proverb)

*K*atya emerged from Grand Central Station into a world surging with an energy that electrified all her senses. New York. The big city. She clutched the handle of her satchel as though it could protect her from the punch of the city's onslaught.

New York City at the beginning of the 20th century

"You don't frighten me," she told the American mega-metropolis. "I'll conquer you!"

"Atta girl!" a passing policeman cheered.

Katya dodged her way through the crowded streets, angling toward the Hudson River. As she turned west on Charles Street, she found the first goal of her walk— a source of shelter. Ma Murphy's Boarding House for Girls. Mr. Murphy captained a tugboat; his wife ran the boarding house. It looked safe, and the two boarders' rooms had the bare necessities: beds, washstands with basins and pitchers, two wooden chairs per room, a couple of old dressers, and nails on the walls for clothes.

There were three beds in a room, two boarders to a bed. Half the girls worked the night shift, half the day. Ma Murphy rented only to laundresses. She told Katya where to find a job on 14th Street.

Inside an hour, Katya had a job. The hitch was that it paid less than the twelve dollars a week she had earned at Eaton's.

"It's okay," she told herself. "This is just a beginning."

In the cavernous laundry room, Katya sat on a high stool in front of a squat gray ironing machine, a cutout copy of a hundred other machines lined up in rows like over-sized school desks. A hundred other girls sat on stools like hers, turning levers this way and that, pressing damp sheets into dry ones.

By the time Katya returned to Ma Murphy's, the night shift had already left for work. She fell into bed, drained of energy and emotion. Being so far away from Georgy sat in her bones as a dull ache.

Within a few weeks, the ghost of starvation returned to haunt Katya. Not only did she not make enough money to send some home, she barely earned enough to stay alive. Hunger pushed her into a decision. She packed her valise and left the laundry and Ma Murphy's to look for a job in a restaurant.

Katya entered every hole-in-the-wall diner full of hope, and left each one deflated. Within a week, her meager savings evaporated, and her new landlady wouldn't let her back in her room without money to pay for the night. Katya retrieved her satchel, and trudged down one block after another without finding employment of any kind. Evening closed in. The crowds thinned. Men she didn't know eyed her.

Katya scanned the tops of buildings for a cross, the sign of Christian hospitality. Sometime after ten o'clock, she spotted the hoped-for cross atop a large brick building. With renewed energy she ascended the cement steps to the landing and rang the bell. A tall, angular portress in a long black habit opened the door.

"Sister," Katya began, "I'm very tired. Could you give me a little corner where I can sleep on the floor? Tomorrow, I'll be able to make other arrangements, but tonight I'm so tired."

"We don't take in strays," the portress snapped, and slammed the door.

Dazed, Katya trudged down the steps to the sidewalk. If those representing Christ wouldn't take her in, where could she go? She walked on, her feet as numb as her heart.

On the Brooklyn Bridge, Katya leaned over the railing and stared at the East River. The dark water, with the city lights reflected on its surface, called to her. Katya leaned farther over the railing.

"What's the use?" the gentle ripples seemed to say. "You can't bring up your son the way you should. Your husband is probably lost to you. Those in the church don't want you. But my waters are welcoming. I'll rock you to sleep—a restful, lasting sleep."

Katya found a space between the cables of the bridge suspension, slipped through, and took a deep breath. Looking down, she cried out, and pressed back against the cables. Mirrored on the water, the face of Christ gazed up at her.

Fighting back through the wires, Katya fled from the bridge. She ran until, gasping for breath, she slowed to a walk. As dawn eased blacks into grays, she discovered she had made her way to the Bowery. Too tired to take another step, she stopped and tried to push down the fear that threatened to overpower her.

"Hey, Blondie," a man called out as she peered into a bakery, "why is your nose pressed against that window? Are you hungry?"

"Yes," Katya admitted.

The stranger took her into a nearby restaurant, where Katya ate two full breakfasts. The man, whom she now knew to be a Jewish taxi driver, paid the bill.

"Come on," he said, and led her to his taxi. "The Mrs. will take care of you."

"Yeah, sure," Katya thought. "Here it is. The only free cheese is in the mousetrap." A chill slithered down her spine, but she was too tired and heartless to fight. She climbed into the taxi.

The driver took her home, and sure enough, his wife, as short, simple and kind as her husband, put her to bed.

Katya slept for over twenty-four hours; and after another hearty breakfast, this one fixed by "the Mrs.", she went with the taxi driver to a restaurant where he knew the owner. In five minutes, Katya had a job as a waitress.

Chapter 15

Nomad

*"The Lord has given me
The grace of restless feet
And hungry heart.
I cannot rest—because
I must follow my Love."*

(Katya: "The Song of a Pilgrim")

That summer of 1924, Katya saw more food than she could have wished for. No better-paying job than waitressing materialized. Tired and discouraged, she returned to Toronto as poor as she had left it.

Holding her small son in her arms again lifted Katya's spirits. Boris was another matter. He had started his own architectural consulting firm, but had set Claudia up in a nearby apartment and ignored the pile of bills. Katya's only hope of paying back the seventy-five dollars he had taken from the charity bazaar lay in her upcoming job with Chautauqua Canada.

Katya and a friend, Chautauqua

In spite of Marietta La Dell's confidence in her, Katya looked with trepidation at the big white canvas tent set up in an open field outside the nickel-mining town of Sudbury, Ontario. She had been told that a Chautauqua speaker had to compete with cows mooing in a neighboring pasture, trains thundering past the tents, cars being cranked up, and babies crying. For that, she was ready, thanks to the practice she'd had bellowing out orders on the food plat-

form at the Front. Wearing a simple homemade black dress, Katya walked out to the center of the recently-constructed stage in the big tent.

"I was brought up on a farm too," she boomed out to her rural audience of several hundred. "I didn't stay on the farm very long, though, because my father's insurance business and his unofficial work as a diplomat took us to many other parts of Europe."

Katya and another friend, Chautauqua Canada

With trembling knees and sweating palms, Katya moved from her introduction to her experiences of Bolshevik raids and her exile from her homeland. The memories brought her to tears. To her astonishment, the engrossed listeners cried with her.

Katya switched to her Russian costume for the audience participation session. A barrage of questions came in rapid succession. When Katya finally left the stage, she was so relieved to be finished that the extended applause almost escaped her.

The next time she stepped onto the platform, though, hecklers drowned out her words. Rotten tomatoes flew at her. She

Katya in her homemade Russian costume, Chautauqua

couldn't dodge them all. The red juice slid down her face and dress. The local Communists had discovered her. Bouncers removed them; but their taunts rang in Katya's ears. She ran backstage to change into her Russian costume and regain her composure. When she returned to the stage, the audience greeted her with a thundering round of applause.

As a lecturer, Katya soon drew high praise from the press as well as her audiences. In a letter to Boris, Marietta La Dell wrote,

"The Baroness has quite outstripped my highest expectations. . . . She charmed everyone with her bigness of soul and gift of understanding the hungry people who

. . . never expected such a wholesome, bright, optimistic personality as Baroness de Hueck radiates on and off the platform."

In 1925, Katya lectured for the United States Chautauqua tour. On the road, she often boarded at people's houses so as to save money on lodging. She sent every spare penny home, to help pay the backlog of bills and keep George well taken care of. Then she found out Boris spent all the money, let the bills pile up higher, and lost their home on Nairn Avenue. He, George, and Dunya had moved to a smaller place on Queen Street, and then to an even smaller one on St. Joseph's. Katya had to fight against a return bout of hopelessness.

Her spiritual director, Fr. John Filion, wrote from Toronto,

"I believe . . . it is God's way of bringing you nearer to Him and preparing you for the great work He has in store for you."

Katya took heart. Her days on the Chautauqua circuit ended, but Archbishop McNeil and another Toronto priest, Fr. George Daly, arranged for her to work as a lecturer for the Catholic Union. That meant going back to New York. As soon as she could find an apartment there, she planned to bring George and, hopefully, Boris too.

When she arrived in the city, in 1926, Katya found it boiling over with literary, musical and artistic creativity springing out of Harlem. On the long walk between the Catholic Union office and the room she shared in Greenwich Village with a struggling actress, Katya passed nightclubs displaying posters of Harlem celebrities: Duke Ellington, an aspiring young pianist. A trumpet player named Louis Armstrong. Eubie Blake, the inspiration behind the first all-Black hit Broadway musical, "Shuffle Along". Posters advertised poetry readings by

Claude McKay, Harlem Renaissance poet

Langston Hughes and Claude McKay. Advertisements promoted dramatic readings by a woman named Zora Neale Hurston.

The creative energy delighted Katya's artistic sensibilities; but it couldn't put food in her mouth. She sent so much money home to Toronto and to her family in Belgium that during a lax time in the lecture business, she had to take a job as a salad girl in a sandwich shop. Bemoaning their fate one morning, she and her roommate sat at the kitchen table pooling their resources. A knock sounded at the door; and Katya got up to answer it. A strange man pushed his way into the room.

"Empty your purses, girls," he ordered.

Langston Hughes, Harlem Renaissance Poet. Photo: Carl Van Vechten

Katya laughed. "Don't bother. They're already empty."

The would-be thief stared at the pitiful pile of change on the table. "Is that all you've got?"

"Yep." Katya shrugged; and her roommate nodded.

"Come on," the man said. "I'll buy you breakfast."

Bolstered by such acts of kindness, and inspired by her work with the Catholic Union, Katya felt a growing desire to let go of everything else and work full-time for the Church, without pay. Pure foolishness, she told herself. But every time she pushed the dream aside, it circled back with mounting force. Katya kept trying to shake it aside. How could she hold onto such an impractical dream?

Her hope of bringing George and Boris to New York started to seem like an impossible dream too. Boris had continued to ignore the ever-growing pile of bills; and he had moved Claudia into their home on St. Joseph Street. When Katya got the news, she felt something snap inside her. The forgiveness and acceptance she had always been able to call forth in prayer evaporated. In a cold rage of rebellion, she took to spending long hours at dances and nightclubs.

Chapter 16

The Hound of Heaven

"I fled Him, down the nights and down the days;
I fled Him, down the arches of the years;
I fled Him, down the labyrinthine ways
Of my own mind and in the mist of tears
I hid from Him, and under running laughter."

(Francis Thompson: "The Hound of Heaven")

Fyodor Chaliapin

Trying to drown her pain in the waters of music and dance, Katya flitted from one jazz club to another, often with Boris's cousin, Colonel George von Hueck, at her side. One evening in Greenwich Village, she heard a familiar song wafting through the open doorway of a dimly lit nightclub. Thinking someone had put on a Russian record, she urged Colonel George inside. The singing broke off; and Fyodor Chaliapin, cried out,

"A Russian! A beautiful Russian! I will sing to you alone."

For the next hour, Chaliapin, in America drawing sell-out crowds at the Metropolitan Opera, sang Russian arias and love songs to Katya. During that hour, all her pain and loneliness fell away. Chaliapin transported her back home to the St. Petersburg of her youth. This man, who Arturo Toscanini once said was the greatest operatic talent with whom he had ever worked, sang life back into Katya.

Morning brought her back to the world of speaking engagements. The lecture business had picked up; and Katya spent late 1926 and early 1927 touring the east coast with the newly-formed Catholic Near East Welfare Association and the Leigh-Emmerich Lecture Bureau. As she always had, she spoke out against recognition of the USSR and Communism.

"Be careful," an old business friend of her father's warned. "You could be in danger."

Katya dismissed Andre Kalpaschnikoff's warning, until a stranger came to her apartment. The man said he was a commercial attaché at the Russian mission. He threatened her life if she didn't stop speaking out against Communism.

As soon as he left, Katya called Mr. Kalpaschnikoff. He hired a bodyguard; and for the next three days, the bodyguard followed Katya everywhere. His constant presence unnerved her more than the Communist had. She called Mr. Kalpaschnikoff again.

"I can't breathe," she told him. "Get this agent off my back!"

She tried to get God off her back too. It didn't work. With each attempt, her spirit grew more restless. She traveled to Garrison, New York, to make a retreat with her friend, Fr. Paul Wattson of Graymoor Monastery. While there, she became a member of the Franciscan Third Order, which committed her to living St. Francis's spirit of poverty and simplicity.

Katya in her lecture costume for Leigh-Emmerich Lecture Bureau

Since praise for her lectures tended to turn Katya's head, she prayed, too, for humility, hiddenness, and childlikeness.

The arrival of George and Boris in New York gave Katya new hope and energy. She pushed her spiritual restlessness to the back burner, giving first place to her improving relationship with Boris. At the same time, Franz Emmerich, co-director of the Leigh-Emmerich Lecture Bureau, asked her to switch from being a lecturer to being an executive.

For her first executive job, Katya had to take charge of Count Hermann Keyserling, a German philosopher and lecturer. Franz said he didn't know anyone besides Katya with a big enough worldview to manage the brilliant universal thinker. The Count believed in a planetary culture that would incorporate all national and ethnic backgrounds, and validate all non-western cultures and philosophies. He claimed that the present age showed the gradual rise and predominance of women all over the world, and that women wanted, not equality, but supremacy, especially in America.

The Count also felt that life in the present age had lost all meaning, and that, as a result, man had lost the will to live, and had developed a suicidal inclination. The only way to check the demolition of all existence and turn it into a new reconstructive process, he felt, would be to give a new significance to life. He said that the key to developing this new significance was to "take from none, and give something to each."

Katya had to organize the eccentric philosopher's schedule down to the minute, and smoothe the ruffled feathers of the reporters he angered with his arrogance. She had to make sure he got on the right train at the right time, and that he had proper clothing for the season. She had to spend a great deal of time listening to him. That was both fascinating and draining.

The rest of Katya's energies went into her life at home. Boris got a job with a Montreal firm, and on February 1, 1928, he left for Quebec. During his absence, Katya spent as much time with George as possible, worked at the lecture bureau, exercised at the gym, stuck to a healthy diet, and worked on her spiritual exercises. She looked forward to her upcoming "celebrity-buying" trip to Europe to search out lecturers for the following season. The trip would allow her to spend more time with George; and Boris planned to meet them in Belgium.

Katya's returning love for Boris received a new blow when he called from Montreal at the beginning of April and told her he worried about the stirrings of his heart. Katya's own heart sank.

Trying not to let her hopes unravel, Katya ignored her fears and looked again at her spiritual life. The restlessness she had been experiencing kept growing stronger. She wanted to recapture the joy of her childhood desire to be voluntarily poor like St. Francis; but her work at Leigh-Emmerich had brought her into financial comfort. What should she do with her nice furniture, good books, and prized record collection?

Finally, worn out from her struggle to live for God in the rarified atmosphere of counts, authors, and world renowned lecturers, Katya decided to abandon her spiritual quest. Boris was right to scorn her wish to live a life of selfless Gospel service. She would become an ordinary, everyday Catholic. Anything more cost too much. She tried to put the restlessness behind her.

Instead of going away, it intensified.

Meanwhile, Katya prepared for her trip abroad.

Katya, possible passport
photo c. 1926

Chapter 17

Arise and Go

*"Sell all you possess and give the money to the poor.
Then come and follow Me."*

(The Gospel of St. Luke)

Count Hermann Keyserling,
philosopher and lecturer

*K*atya's first meeting with her mother and brothers in Brussels horrified her. In spite of all the help she sent them, they still lived in dire poverty. Serge, now twenty-three and studying agriculture at Louvain, and Andrew, a budding teenager, seemed like strangers with whom she had nothing in common.

Lonely and sad, Katya went to Darmstadt, Germany, to see Count Keyserling and sign him up for another lecture tour. The Bureau needed a good lineup for the next season, because back in New York, the post-war economic slump had Franz Emmerich and his co-director W. Colston Leigh scrambling for financial stability. Franz asked Katya to live as frugally as possible, but to "put up a good appearance before European celebrities."

In between meetings with potential lecturers, Katya worked with the Red Cross in trying to locate Nicholas Makletzoff, whom she hadn't seen since the war. She found out that he had made his way to Sofia, Bulgaria, where he lived near his brother and eked out a bare-bones existence. Alienated from her family and Boris, Katya began writing Nicholas long letters, giving voice to all of her pent up grief. On August 3, 1928, she wrote to him from her mother's apartment in Brussels,

"My life with B. G. [Boris Gidonovich] is tragic and nightmarish."

Katya loved having more time to spend with George, though, and on August 6, she wrote,

"The very best of me has been passed on to him."

A telegram from Leigh-Emmerich stated that Katya should remain in Europe until November or December. Katya was glad. The extra time would give her a chance to see Nicholas and maybe get him out of Bulgaria. She worried that he was dying from within in Sofia. She and Serge worked at finding a job for him in Brussels.

On August 16, two days after Boris arrived in Brussels and the day after Katya's thirty-second birthday, she, Boris, and

Katya and young George, en route

George began a pilgrimage to Kiskile, Finland. They took the train across Belgium to Germany and Poland, and then north to Finland. On the long trip, Boris hardly spoke; and Katya found him "a tedious travel partner."

On August 25, when passing through Vyborg, Finland, Katya wrote about it, "You're dearer to me than ever. Papa is buried there. Was at his grave and wept a long while. My wonderful papa! My dear cherished one. Did you understand how I loved you?"

Outside Kiskile, *Merri-Lokki* looked the same as when Katya had left it ten years before.

"So nice here," she wrote in her diary. "Quiet for the soul and rest for the heart. I love this place; it's dear to me. Still, I feel sad. I can see so clearly here, and it's not a happy picture. I've lost Borya altogether."

Merri-Lokki, 1928, young George in doorway

Soon after Katya, Boris, and George got back to Belgium, Boris, and George sailed to Canada. Katya went to London, where she set up a British branch office and visited with prospective lecturers and authors. A telegram from Franz said that the Bureau had crashed on the rocks of financial disaster. For a moment, Franz wanted Katya to return to New York; but then he changed his mind.

"It is much better for you to stick it out and not have to go back until next summer," he wrote on October 19, 1928.

The stress of her packed schedule, living as a pauper while presenting herself as a princess, and the news that Boris had lost $2,000, put Katya on the road to a nervous breakdown.

"Hell on earth," she wrote in her diary. "Everything goes smash. Good Lord, why? . . . I am so tired, so terribly tired."

Running on a hidden tank of reserve energy, Katya went to Bulgaria to try and sign up the King as a lecturer. He declined; but Katya was able to see Nicholas. She came away from their visit convinced that he was lost in inner darkness and needed to get out of Bulgaria as soon as possible. Sailing back to Canada in January, 1929, she wrote to Nicholas,

"*There is not a single doubt in my soul.* In spite of the difficulties of your struggles with life, despite the darkness, you must go forward."

Aside from seasickness on the rough crossing, Katya found the ocean voyage a good time for solitary stillness. Again, she felt the Lord tapping her on the shoulder. On January 11, still aboard ship, she wrote to Nicholas,

"I must . . . find a quiet place and live there in peace and doing good to others. 'I have come to serve.' That is how I must serve in this world, all men, for the glory of God. Oh, my God, help me to find the right path."

When Katya got home to Montreal, she was appalled to find George pale and thin.

"He was crazy with joy at seeing me," she wrote to Nicholas later in January. "What happiness to hug him and hold him very close to me. You understand, of course, Kolya, and you are happy for me?"

Katya told Nicholas that Boris would help get him out of Bulgaria, and would give him a job as a draftsman in his Montreal business.

Because of the lecture bureau's financial collapse, Katya was free to stay in Montreal, where George needed her. She worked at recuperating from her trip and making sure George got healthier. Her spiritual restlessness kept coming back; and she started consulting Bibles for some sign of the direction she should take in serving others. Every time she opened the Scriptures, she saw the same line:

"Arise, go. Sell all you possess. Take up your cross, and follow Me."

At night, the poor filled Katya's dreams: The laundresses, waitresses, and factory workers with whom she had once shared hunger. Ma Murphy's boarding house for girls. She kept going to the Bible for answers. No matter what translation she picked up, she landed on a similar passage:

"Arise, go. Sell what you possess, give it to the poor, and follow Me."

"That's fine for single people who think they might be called to the priesthood or convent," she thought, "but I have a son!" She tried to push the whole crazy idea out of her mind.

Chapter 18

When God Winks

"When God winks, drop your work and follow Him."
(Russian proverb)

*K*atya tried to shake off her restlessness, but it clung to her more stubbornly than a tick to a dog's ear. The bottom fell out of the stock market. Boris's architectural firm collapsed. Katya couldn't find a job. Still, the desire to follow Christ and serve the poor gnawed at her more than anything else. In January, 1930, to sort things out, she went on a retreat. While on it, knowing she had to get all her relationships in order, she wrote to Nicholas, whom she loved,

"My dear Kolya,

"Our love, in its human reality—we have to lay it down at [the Lord's] feet. ... Our road is long and difficult, beyond human endurance; but God walks with us."

Boris's cruelties became overwhelming.

"Day after day—long night after long night," Katya wrote in her diary, "I face this desire to leave [and go] far from these wounding words, like a sword, far from these humiliating remarks—which leave my soul bleeding. . . . And yet . . . I stay. . . . Why—because . . . Jesus is on the other side [of the cross]. With His grace—I stay. Not for a moment could I do it without Him."

Katya forgave Boris "with all my heart and soul" for the hurt and sorrow he piled on her.

Nicholas Makletzoff, outing near Toronto

It occurred to her that she didn't have to go anywhere else or do anything big in order to live for others. She wrote,

"It all has become suddenly so simple—to seek nothing but what is at hand. My work is Georgy, Boris, his salvation. Nicholas, his sanctification. My home— the task of

Katya, outing near Toronto

keeping it together; and that is all.

"For me, an ordinary life in an extraordinary good way."

The time soon came, though, when Katya felt she could no longer stay with Boris. She began seeking an official separation.

Boris, possibly the same outing

He asked her to make an attempt at reconciliation. She agreed to try, and went with him to their cabin on Lac Castor, in the Laurentian foothills of Quebec. Almost as soon as they arrived at the cottage, Boris's cruelties burst out of him like explosives, killing something in Katya, and ending her life with him.

Only two things now claimed Katya's attention: George, and listening to God's call to become one with the poor. Somehow or another, that's what she had to do.

Ste. Marguerite's cabin, in Quebec

Chapter 19

That Crazy Russian

"The Russian genius, when it has reached a summit, throws itself down and wants to mingle with the earth, and the people."

(Nicholas Berdyaev: *The Russian Idea*)

*K*atya knew that as she worked out a way to be one with the poor, she would need a source of income in order to provide for George. She applied for nurse's training at the Montreal General Hospital, hoping her savings would hold out until she could get through school and find a job in a hospital.

Boris and Claudia fought too much for George to stay with his father while Katya studied. So, Katya sent him to a Jesuit boarding school in Manitoba, which she felt sure would provide a good environment.

Katya's restlessness often rose to the surface during her nursing school days. The poor called to her. On a commuter train ride, she heard a refrain in the rhythm of the wheels: "Be poor—one with them—one with Me. One with them—one with Me."

Some of the diary notes she had written in the past couple of years echoed in her head:

"Be poor. Be simple. Be childlike in trust."

How? Where? Part of the answer came through a series of dilemmas. By September, 1932, after completing her first year in nursing school, Katya found herself drowning in a flood of new scandals surrounding Boris and his mistresses. Old temptations like impatience and a re-awakened desire for good food and good times assailed her. George hadn't liked the school in Manitoba, and he begged not to be sent back there.

Katya consulted with William Sherman and his wife, friends who had a cottage near theirs in Quebec. They said they would be happy to add George to their family ranks. He could go to school with their children, whom he loved. Knowing George would be safe and happy with the Shermans, Katya wrestled with where she should go in order to get away from the scandals, and to avoid spiritual disintegration. George, who would be a part of her vocation, had been born in Toronto. She had first experienced North American poverty in Toronto. Archbishop McNeil, who, she was sure, could guide her, lived in Toronto.

With as much certainty as she could muster, Katya left George in the care of the Shermans and packed for Toronto. She would live in a humble apartment in a poor immigrant district, finish her nurse's training, and spend her spare time caring for sick or overworked neighbors.

Boris ridiculed her. Friends laughed at her. People she didn't know began referring to her as "that crazy Russian."

It hurt, the laughter and the scorn; but Katya had a stronger voice to listen to than those of the skeptics. She left for Toronto in the fall of 1932, and signed up to continue her nursing studies at St. Michael's Hospital School of Nursing. Within a week, she realized hospital work wasn't for her. She went to Archbishop McNeil and told him she wanted to "follow Christ into the modern jungle that is inhabited by the have-nots, the masses, and the forgotten ones, to work without the benefit of a religious habit, become a servant of the poor . . . and battle Communism and all the other 'isms' that corrode man's soul—face to face . . . as Jacob battled the angel."

Not much taller than Katya, but dignified and peaceful, the white-haired, blue-eyed Archbishop suggested she live in Toronto for a year, praying for God's guidance. If, at the end of the year, she was still sure God was calling her to the life of Franciscan poverty, living by begging as he had, the Archbishop would do everything he could to support her.

Archbishop Neil McNeil

He reminded Katya that, although she might be called to poverty, George wasn't. He should always receive good food, medical care, proper clothing, and a good education.

Katya agreed. She had already put money aside for him.

To help her survive during her year of discernment, the Archbishop asked Katya to do a survey of local Communist activities for the diocese. He offered her

$15.00 a week, with an advance of $30.00, and helped her locate a downstairs apartment in a house at 141 Isabella Street.

When Katya went to Montreal to get George, he said he would rather stay with the Shermans and go to school with his friends.

The Shermans were Jewish; and Katya wanted George to become rooted in the Catholic faith. But he loved being with the Shermans; and they provided him with a solid, healthy family life. She told Boris she was in favor of keeping him there.

Boris exploded. "If you don't take him away from there, I will!"

Not wanting to turn George against his father, but not wanting to leave him to his fate with Claudia, Katya brought George to live with her in Toronto, as she had first planned.

Unaware of his parents' conflict, George accused his mother of not wanting him to be happy. He turned belligerent and hard to handle. Katya could only hope he would soon settle down and enjoy his school in Toronto.

In her survey work, Katya infiltrated dozens of Bolshevik gatherings, mostly held in cheap restaurants and labor halls. The Communists targeted the poor immigrants, who flocked to the city for promised work that proved hard to find. Angry and frustrated, they listened to the Communists' claims to win justice for the workers of the world. They didn't realize that when the Communists got into power, they maintained it by keeping the workers downtrodden.

The Communists also targeted the young. Katya wrote in her survey,

"Our youth plunges headlong into that new and exciting role that leads to a life without restrictions, without responsibilities, without moral obligations—a land where there is no God, where everyone, so they think, is free to do as he or she likes."

Katya suggested to Archbishop McNeil that the Church get more involved in high schools, college, and youth groups. She herself lectured to many youth, service and church groups.

Mrs. Beatrice Field, mother of two daughters near George's age, had worked in the slums of London, England. She wanted to help Katya with serving the poor in Toronto. Her friend, Grace Flewelling (Flewy), also wanted to work with the poor. Three other people approached Katya. Kay Kenny, Charlie Rogers, and petite, shy twenty-one-year-old Olga La Plante wanted to help Katya serve the poor.

Not sure what to do with them all, Katya decided they should form a study club to learn about the spirituality of St. Francis and study Scripture, liturgy, and the Popes' encyclicals on social justice.

"If you're going to serve the poor," she said, "then you need a strong spiritual foundation on which to build your work."

Many of the new Russian immigrants asked Katya to help them find work. The Depression, or "the Dirty Thirties," as it was called in Canada, had robbed many of their jobs.

Building on a couple people's ability to cook, Katya suggested starting a Russian restaurant. She begged the money to rent a house, pots and pans, linoleum and wallpaper. Musicians tuned up their balalaikas. Nicholas came from Montreal to plaster the inside walls of the restaurant, paint Russian-style murals on them, and make wooden nesting dolls to sell to the diners.

Adjacent to the restaurant, Katya's newly-formed group opened a dress-making shop and a beauty salon.

Advertisement poster by Nicholas Makletzoff

Frederick Griffin, a reporter for the *Toronto Star* newspaper, wrote an article on December 9, 1933, describing thirty-seven-year-old Katya as "a vital, youthful, if mature woman who is an outstanding leader. . . . There is wisdom in this woman who has suffered, fought, lived; courage and strength. . . . She has seen the sullen spread of despair among the submerged, right in Toronto."

And the Communists had seen her at too many of their meetings. They grew suspicious.

Chapter 20

A House of Friendship

"Man is great when he serves others—even if the others do not notice how much effort is being put out on their behalf."

(Katya, 1933)

*K*atya infiltrated a Communist meeting at a downtown speakeasy. As usual, factory workers, maids, store clerks, students, and disillusioned immigrants made up most of the audience. Katya sat with them, and listened to the sweet-sounding but empty promises for a rosy future for all downtrodden workers.

Shortly before ten o'clock, she left the speakeasy and started walking home. By the second block, she realized she was being followed.

Not again! Pretending she hadn't noticed anything, Katya walked a little farther, and then slipped into a dark alleyway. She doubled back to Mrs. Field's apartment, where she had left George in her friend's care.

A distraught Mrs. Field met Katya in the kitchen with the news that George had disappeared again. He and her two girls had been playing hide and seek; and George had evaporated.

Her heart in her throat, Katya told Mrs. Field not to worry. George would come back in a few days. He always did.

Later, in bed but sleepless, Katya wasn't so sure. George was only twelve. He could be in trouble way over his head. What could she do to change this terrible pattern? No answer came; but in a few days George did come home, acting as though nothing unusual had happened. A couple months went by without a recurrence, and Katya allowed herself to concentrate on her work again. She began a Catholic Youth Group, an adult spiritual life group for those out of work, and helped find jobs.

Olga, Flewy, Charlie Rogers and Kay Kenny approached Katya, saying they wanted to form a more serious bond with her and her work.

Speechless, Katya went to Archbishop McNeil.

"Mine is a solitary vocation," she said. "My dream has always been to live and pray in the *poustinia*, the desert, and go to the people when they need a helping hand."

The Archbishop said God must be asking her to be the foundress of a group. She should accept the others into her dream.

Knowing she had to obey, Katya accepted them. She called the new little group the Guild of Our Lady of Atonement, patterned after Fr. Paul Wattson's Franciscan Friars of the Atonement in Graymoor, New York.

Archbishop McNeil said that another thing Katya needed to do was go to New York City and meet a woman named Dorothy Day. He said Dorothy published a news-

paper called the *Catholic Worker,* with articles about social justice that echoed the way Katya talked. He handed
her the funds for the trip.

Katya took the next train
to New York; and returned
to Toronto knowing she had
found a soul mate. The lean,
soft-spoken but determined
Dorothy, so unlike her own
robust, flamboyant, forceful
self, believed too that a person had to become one with
the poor, one with Christ.

Energized by her visit
with Dorothy, and buoyed by
Archbishop McNeil's blessing, Katya opened what she
called a Friendship House. She found an empty building on Portland Street, and begged the money to rent a
room that had a storefront window on the main floor.

Friendship House Toronto storefront

In starting up her new group apostolate, Katya worried most about one thing: how could she be a good
enough example for the others? She had to try harder to
live what she preached, so as not to be a scandal to those
with whom she worked.

The Depression
determined the first
in-house work of her
Friendship House. An
unemployed wanderer
appeared at the door,
asking for food. Katya
and her helpers fed him
lunch. The next day,

Katya in Toronto Friendship House, with
Mr. Gold, her secretary

nearly twenty came. Soon, an average of one hundred and fifty homeless men showed up on a regular basis.

In need of food for so many hungry patrons, Katya soon drained the meager amount of donated funds Friendship House had in the Bank of Montreal. Bespectacled Mr. Krafchek, the manager of the bank that sat kitty-corner from the storefront, sighed and told Katya the account was overdrawn by one hundred dollars.

In her defense, Katya took Mr. Krafchek across the street for a tour. She showed him the lineup of about a hundred people outside the St. Francis storefront, waiting for their turn to eat. She showed the banker another lineup outside St. Theresa's Clothing Room storefront.

Moved by what he saw, Mr. Krafchek covered the overdraft himself; and he and the employees in the bank took up a collection and sent Katya apples and oranges for the Friendship House Christmas baskets.

Such wonderful friends and benefactors made Katya

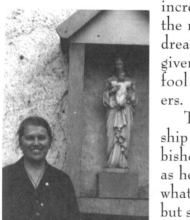

Katya and her backyard shrine, Our Lady of Atonement

increasingly sure she was on the right track in following the dream she perceived God had given her, even though He did fool her by bringing in co-workers.

Through all of her Friendship House adventures, Archbishop McNeil helped as much as he could. Katya didn't know what she would do without him; but soon she had to find out. In May, 1934, the Archbishop fell sick. As he lay dying in the hospital, he called Katya to his side.

"If you're faithful," he said, "your houses of friendship will cover this continent and spill to other lands. You will know much pain and darkness for a long time; but be faithful to God and His Mother."

The Archbishop died on May 25, 1934; and Katya had to carry on without his fatherly support.

On June 23, she and the members of her Guild of Our Lady of Atonement made what she called "First Promises of Friendship House". She prayed that she would spend the rest of her life in God's service, "not to gain heaven, not to escape hell, but because I love You!" She hoped she would never count what it cost her to serve God in that way.

The Guild grew in membership; and Friendship House celebrated its official opening on September 14. By the end of October, Katya quailed under the load of leadership and the loneliness that always accompanies one in authority.

As foundress of the Catholic Worker, Dorothy Day understood how Katya felt; and the two pioneers in Catholic social justice became fast friends.

Fr. Henry Carr, Superior General of the Toronto-based Basilian Order of Priests, also understood Katya and her mission. He became the spiritual guide for the members of the fledgling Guild and its outreach of Friendship House.

When a second Friendship House opened in Ottawa, Katya wrote to Fr. Carr,

"It is wonderful how God is good, if you are just willing to be patient and suffer and suffer and suffer."

Katya's suffering had barely begun. One day, out of the blue, a Sister stood at the front of her classroom and told the children to pray for the Baroness, who was sending stolen money to the Communists in Russia.

Chapter 21

The Big Trouble

"Always we have stoned the prophets."

(Mary Ward, Friendship House volunteer)

*T*he rumors struck as hard and fast as mortar shells, scattering shrapnel that cut Katya to pieces. She went to church as usual, but when she sat down, everyone else in her pew got up and moved to another one. At the grocery store, an old friend stuck her face in front of Katya's, and snarled,

"Traitor! Communist spy!"

Katya ran outside. Unseeing, she rushed down Spadina Avenue.

"Get out of here!" a plumber who had gotten his job through Katya screamed, and spit at her.

Katya spun around, and hurried in the direction from which she had come. When she reached the city limits, she collapsed onto the grass by the road.

"If I could only die! If my heart and I could only die!"

After a long time, Katya pushed herself to her feet and trudged back into town. In the dark cavern of an almost deserted movie theater, she sat motionless until the building closed, and the usher kicked her out.

Frightened and sleepless, Katya waded through the days, until, finally, the fatal blow struck. On November 25, 1936, she wrote to Fr. Carr,

"The Archbishop [James McGuigan] has spoken, and Friendship House is no more.

"I am accused of:

"i Being a Communist worker from within

"ii Having absconded with Friendship House money

"iii Being an immoral and unworthy character

"iv Seducing priests

"v Being a Communist spy

". . . All around me are laying the remnants of my life; and I am a 'failure' in the eyes of the world."

Katya wouldn't say anything against the Sister who started the rumors, or against the priests who believed and spread them. She felt that to speak out against religious and clergy would be to speak out against the Church, the Bride of Christ. Her conviction robbed her of any defense she might have had.

Fr. Carr stood by her. He wrote,

"Your tireless energy, your enthusiasm and zeal, your brilliant ability and outstanding knowledge, no one can question them. Whatever mistakes you have made, whatever your faults, you have been working with all your soul for God's holy church. He will not abandon you."

Bewildered and lost, Katya faced the instant switch from a life of tremendous activity to one of doing almost nothing. The former stream of visitors dried up. Her once heavy lecture schedule dissolved. When the rare person knocked on her door, Katya was afraid to answer it.

Falling into despondency, she couldn't muster up the energy to get interested in anything, until she happened to pick up a copy of *Fire on the Earth* by Fr. Paul Hanley Furfey, a Catholic professor in Washington, D. C. His book promoted racial equality throughout the Church. Katya wanted to talk with this priest whose insistence on living Christianity without compromise sounded so much like her desire to preach the Gospel with her whole life.

Every time Katya left home, chills and tremors wracked her body; so how could she go to Washington to talk with Fr. Furfey? It took until March, 1937, for her to gather enough courage to go and meet him. As they talked, her heart leaped at the possibilities for Catholic lay action in bringing social justice to the poor and the outcast.

As encouraging as the visit was, Katya still had to deal with her own battles. Besides the ongoing rumors and the breaking up of Friendship House, she had to face the effects of the Depression. Horrific economic conditions and fear stretched her nerves and resources. Since her writing and editing work for her recently founded newspaper, *Social Forum*, didn't bring in enough revenue to keep her going, she took Fr. Carr's suggestion to go to New York and see Dorothy Day.

Katya and Dorothy Day at the Catholic Worker

Dorothy, Peter Maurin, Stanley Vishnewski, and several Catholic Worker volunteers met her at their front door on Mott Street, singing the "Hymn to Confessors", in honor of the suffering she had endured for the Gospel. Tears welled up in Katya's eyes; and as soon as she stepped inside the door of the Catholic Worker House, her chills and tremors fell away.

In New York, Fr. Theophane McGuire, editor for the *Sign* magazine, asked Katya if she would go abroad as a foreign correspondent and write a series of articles on Catholic Action in Europe.

Glad for some immediate, if not long-lasting, direction in her life, Katya accepted Fr. McGuire's assignment. She returned to Toronto to prepare for the trip. While she cleared up some loose ends, Nicholas told her about his recent adventures. He had discovered a small, quiet bay on the Madawaska River, nearly two hundred miles northeast of Toronto. An abundance of pike, bass, and perch populated the river. Nicholas was hooked. He bought five acres of land on the bay, and the island property next to it. He was building a small Russian-style *izba* on the island.

Katya was happy for Nicholas; and she looked forward to her own travels. As she packed to leave, though, fifteen-year-old George, who had been staying with Boris and Claudia in Montreal, ran away from them. Nobody had a clue where he had gone. Devastated, Katya decided to cancel her trip.

Flewy, Olga, and Mrs. Field objected.

"You have to continue with your plans," Mrs. Field said. "If George shows up in Toronto, we'll take care of him."

Katya hesitated; but she knew they were right. She couldn't be of any help to George, and she needed to fulfill her commitment to Fr. McGuire. On one of many sleepless nights, she wrote a letter to George that she knew he may never see:

"I shall go into distant lands with the terrible burden of no certainty about you. All I have left is prayer. It alone will be our bond."

Katya sailed for England from Montreal on June 4, 1937. She took with her two main prayer intentions: George's safety and the will to love, as well as forgive, her persecutors in Toronto.

In Brussels, Katya went to visit her mother, and found out that George had been beaten and left for dead in a boxcar in the United States. When he regained consciousness, he called his father and begged to be allowed to come home. Boris gave him one option—boarding school in

Katya working on her articles in Portugal

L to R: George, Katya's brother Serge, Katya in Belgium

England—which he would reach by working his way across the ocean on a cattle boat. George agreed; and on August 28, 1937, Boris traveled to England on a luxury liner to prepare for George's acceptance at Clayes Boarding School, in Dorset. George arrived soon after his father; and Katya met them at the English dock. She made arrangements for George to stay with newly-married Serge or Andrew and their wives in Belgium during school breaks.

Katya returned to Canada in much better psychological and physical condition than when she had left it, but still uncertain about the future. The months away from Toronto hadn't lessened the impact of the false rumors. Accusing glances and cold shoulders brought back her

L-R: Katya's brother Andrew, his wife Sarita, Katya, a friend, Anita, George, another friend

tremors and chills. She decided to return to New York to be near Dorothy Day.

At the Catholic Worker, Katya connected with her old friend, Fr. John LaFarge, who worked in interracial justice. He suggested Katya open a Friendship House in Harlem.

The thought of it sent shivers down Katya's spine; but she picked herself up, bandaged her newly opened wounds, and started her life all over again.

Chapter 22

Harlem, Wherein Katya Becomes a Battering Ram

"You're on a lonely crusade to break down the racial prejudices of America."

(Stanley Vishnewski to Katya)

*T*he subway train roared into the 135th Street station; and Katya rose from her seat. Lugging a paper shopping bag stuffed with tattered towels, washcloths, and sheets, she climbed the littered cement stairs to the winter-barren street. Stanley, the teenage Catholic Worker volunteer Dorothy Day had asked to help Katya, carried her cardboard suitcase in one hand and her well worn Remington typewriter in the other.

The previous day, February 14, 1938, Katya had rented and moved into a little Harlem apartment. It hadn't been easy finding a place. Footsore and frustrated at the end of a long day's fruitless search, Katya had blurted out to one landlord that she had never encountered such racial prejudice in Russia. The man, who owned a three-story walkup at 138th Street and Lenox

Ellen Tarry, children's story hour

Ann Harrigan

Building containing FH storefront

Ellen Tarry

Martin de Porres Lending Library, W 135th Street

Avenue, thought that meant she was a Communist; and he rented to her on the spot.

Harlem backyard basket maker

In spite of her fears about starting another Friendship House, Katya looked forward to her new work. Like the refugees in Toronto, many of Harlem's residents had come to New York from elsewhere, mostly from the South and the Caribbean. She was about to meet a brand new group of struggling immigrants. Almost all of the local Harlem markets and stores were owned and operated by white people who lived outside the district. They hired African-American help at a pay rate of less than subsistence level. Colleges and universities kept their doors closed against Black students. Mothers had to travel downtown to clean, cook, and sew in rich people's houses for long hours, little time off, and less pay than that of the store clerks. The whole deplorable situation "stuck in my craw," as Katya put it in her ever-developing American slang. Where was

New York skyline from bridge, 1920s

the Catholic Church in this hotbed of injustice? Katya meant to find answers to that question.

She led Stanley up the dark stairwell of the tenement building to her room. She put her shopping bag on the floor, and pinned a magazine picture from her scuffed brown leather purse onto the wall. Blessed Martin de Porres was the perfect patron for the new Friendship House. He was a half-black, half-white, 16th century Peruvian Dominican Brother who suffered from prejudice, poverty, and a lack of schooling. In spite of all that, he became a great healer of body and soul for thousands of people, black and white. With him in place, Katya told Stanley, she was at home.

As Stanley wrote later, he nodded in agreement, but remained doubtful. He glanced at the helter-skelter pile of newspapers in the corner of the room. Not much of a bed.

When Stanley left, Katya crossed the street to meet Fr. Michael Mulvoy, pastor of St. Mark's Parish. To Katya's wonder and relief, he felt the same way she did about the need to break down the barriers of prejudice. The tall, redheaded Irishman found jobs for scores of his parishioners, and for others who needed his help to cross the color line of prejudice. Katya's neighbors referred to him as "the blackest white man in Harlem."

Fr. Michael Mulvoy

Energized by meeting a like-spirited friend, Katya plunged into her work. Before she had a bed or a dresser, she had a lecture schedule.

"Our enemy is complacency!" Katya shouted from speakers' platforms all over New York City and beyond. She hit the Catholics the hardest.

Thomas Merton became a Friendship House volunteer as a result of hearing her at St. Bonaventure College, in upstate New York. In his autobiography, *Seven Storey Mountain*, he said that Katya cried out to an audience of mostly priests and nuns,

"Communism would make very little progress in the world or none at all, if Catholics really lived up to their obligations, and did the things Christ came on earth to teach them to do: that is, if they really loved one another, and saw Christ in one another, and did something to win justice for the poor."

A woman who lived on Park Avenue asked Katya to speak to a small group of women at her home.

Friendship House Harlem storefronts

Busy opening storefronts on 135th Street, starting youth groups and study clubs, a library and a clothing room, Katya didn't give the talk much thought until one day she checked her calendar and realized she had to be at the woman's home that very afternoon. She didn't have a coat worthy of the name; and she had to travel in sub-zero weather. Scrounging through the clothing room donations, she found one coat. It looked like it was made from a squirrel that had lost a fight to a raccoon. Katya threw it on, caught the bus, and arrived at her destination bearing the resemblance of a hunter checking his trap lines.

The butler who opened the door looked at her with obvious disapproval, and took her coat as though it were a live vermin. He held it as far from him as he could while working it onto a hanger.

The hostess arrived at Katya's elbow. Fussing over whether everything was ready for the gathering, she didn't notice the coat. She led Katya into the drawing room, and introduced her to the other women seated on divans and stuffed chairs.

Katya gave what she hoped was an animated and convincing lecture about social and interracial justice, begging in the spirit of St. Francis, and the work of Friendship House. Afterward, she had tea and cookies with the club members. Then came the time to go home.

Her entrance scene repeated itself in reverse. The butler took her coat with the thumb and forefinger of each hand, and started to help Katya into it. Still in his hands, the coat fell apart down the middle—two squirrels instead of one.

Katya turned to her hostess. "Like I was telling you, we wear second-hand clothes; and we try to give the best things to the poor."

For the first time, the butler smiled.

"There's nothing to be done," the hostess said. "We'll send you back in my car."

When the Rolls Royce pulled up to the curb in front of the Friendship House library, everybody rushed out to see what was up.

Katya stepped out, waved goodbye to the driver, hello to the crowd, and, since she no longer had a coat, hurried inside.

In the spring, Katya gave a lecture on interracial justice at a nearby Brooklyn parish. After her talk, she asked for clothing donations. A few days later, a stunning black-haired, blue-eyed teacher named Ann Harrigan arrived with a friend at Katya's apartment. They handed her a box of clothing, said how much they had enjoyed her talk, and left. Before long, Ann came back to volunteer after school and on weekends. A painful childhood had made relationships difficult for her, but she believed in what Friendship House was doing, and wanted to become a part of it.

Soon, other volunteers appeared. Their numbers grew, and several became full-time Friendship House Staff Workers. Flewy came from Toronto. In her early fifties now, with gray hair and gray eyes, she held the position of the oldest staff worker. She could, at times, challenge Katya's patience, but Katya loved and counted on her. She excelled in what Katya called "the chit-chat apostolate", making friends with everyone she met.

Katya doing correspondence

Even with Flewy there, the other staff and volunteers always around, and neighbors coming and going all day, Katya couldn't dispel an abiding loneliness. She missed the few friends she had left in Canada. She wished she could be closer to her mother and family in Belgium, where political unrest undermined the whole European social structure. Under it all lurked the pain of her Toronto experience.

"We are in Harlem, my heart and I," Katya wrote. "The spittle of Toronto. The curious eyes. The dirty hands that tear into the soul. They will return. Shall I pack again, my heart? Shall I walk again—and walk—and walk? Shall we go away, my heart, so we will not hurt these shining kids?"

It didn't help that many of the clergy and hierarchy got threatened and angered by the unheard-of apostolic work of a laywoman. Katya wondered if she should quit fighting them, and give up. In May, 1938, she wrote,

"How hard it is to work where those who should lead us do not, and those who should help do not care."

Katya urged the people of Harlem not to wait for others to come and help them, but to form their own cooperatives and credit unions.

Writer Ellen Tarry, a friend of Fr. Mulvoy, introduced Katya to some of her other friends, mostly writers of the Harlem Renaissance. When some of them complained about how their lives had been ruined because they couldn't display their talents in the white world, Katya prodded them too.

"Don't accept defeat. Help yourselves. Get to work; and don't give up!"

She invited poets Claude McKay and Langston Hughes to come to Friendship House to read their writings and give workshops.

At the same time, she convinced many white publishers and gallery owners to wake up to the unique talent of Harlem artists.

During the first year of her new apostolate, Katya saw Harlem hit the international news headlines when, on June 22, 1938, Joe Louis won the world heavyweight boxing championship.

"All Harlem went wild," Katya wrote that night. "Louis won in the first round, and put Schmelling to sleep!"

By September of that year, the headlines bore more ominous news. Hitler took over one section of the fragmented Czechoslovakia; and in his greed for power, he grew hungry for more.

"Wake up!" Katya cried out from the lecture platform. "The complacency of Christians has fostered the atmosphere that allows for those like Hitler to rise to power. Now is the time to begin to love, to begin to serve, burning with zeal and charity. Tomorrow may be too late!"

First Communion Class

Chapter 23

A Voice Crying in the Wilderness

"I heard the voice of God:
'Arise, oh prophet, watch and hearken,
And with my Will thy soul engird,
Roam the gray seas, the roads that darken,
And burn men's hearts with this, my Word.'"

(Alexander Pushkin: excerpt from "The Prophet")

While England, France, and Russia mobilized for war, Katya dealt with her own conflicts in Harlem. At a fancy dinner, where she had been seated at the head table with a Cardinal and other dignitaries, she asked the Cardinal to accept a gifted boy from Harlem into a Catholic college in his diocese.

"How can I?" he said. "A lot of wealthy benefactors would withdraw their funding. How would we pay our huge mortgage?"

"If you don't accept him," Katya blurted out, "what religion will you be teaching at your college? You'll wind up paying for that mortgage twice—once here, and once in hell!"

The Cardinal gasped. Two seconds later, the dinner hostess appeared at Katya's elbow.

"I'm so very sorry, Baroness, that you have to leave for your next engagement. I have a car waiting outside for you."

When Katya got back to Friendship House, she told the staff they might as well start shutting down, they were done for. She had just told a Cardinal he was going to hell.

A death-like pall hung over Friendship House for the next two nerve-wracking days. When the call came, Katya was standing by her desk. She dropped into her chair, before her knees could buckle. The Cardinal's voice crackled over the wires.

Scholarship student Herb McKnight, standing, middle

"B," he said, using her new nickname, "I've decided I only want to pay for that mortgage once. Send us your student."

Katya hung up the phone, pulled out a bottle of scotch she had been given "for medicinal purposes," and downed a big gulp. When she trusted herself to speak, she sent for young Herb McKnight, and told him to start packing for college.[1]

At all of her lectures, Katya demanded to know why no black faces appeared in her audiences. At seminaries and convents, she asked, "Why are black applicants refused?"

All over the South, Katya went from diocese to diocese, urging Bishops to meet the need for racial equality and social justice. In one city, where she gave an open lecture, she asked why there were so many people of mixed blood in the South, while segregation still prevailed.

"If a black is good enough for a white to sleep with," she boomed into the microphone, "then he or she is good enough to marry."

An instantaneous mob surged toward the stage. Katya backed against the curtain.

Hands reached out from backstage and grabbed her. The next thing she knew, she was being shoved into a garbage can and hauled out to the back alley.

"Don't move, Miss Catherine. Don't talk."

Katya recognized the voice of the black stagehand she had met before her talk. She did as instructed, rocking inside her confined quarters as the garbage can rose into the air.

Sweating with fear and the heat, Katya landed with a thud inside what could only be a garbage truck. The crunching of heavy tires on gravel and a sudden jolt told her she had begun an abrupt exit out of town.

---

1 Herb McKnight became a medical doctor; and he and Katya remained friends for many years to come.

Chapter 24

A Journey into Hell

*"When a dog starts barking,
other dogs soon join him."*

(Russian Proverb)

*K*atya's next hazardous trip took her back to Europe in 1939. She saw that George was doing well at school in England; but everyone in Britain seemed to live in fearful expectation of news from Germany. The same nervousness prevailed in Belgium.

In Germany, Katya posed as a visiting social worker, while, at the same time, worked as an undercover reporter. She soon found out that the Third Reich put on a good show for international visitors; but so much money had gone into war preparations that restaurants carried only ersatz coffee and butter. The general populace didn't even have that. Germany boasted of a wonderful social service system network all over the country. Closer investigation in back streets and rural areas exposed the fact that these services were available only for Aryans.

In Munich, Katya saw large numbers of special troops swarm over an area where the Fuehrer was to speak. After hours of waiting in the growing throngs of people, Katya heard trumpets blare. A sea of red and black flags carrying the sign of the swastika appeared above the masses of onlookers.

A little man with a cowlick falling over one eye materialized on the speaker's platform. Adolph Hitler. In a high squeaky voice, he yelled at the top of his lungs about supermen, a super race, and the right of the Germans to clear the country of undesirables.

Katya's stomach heaved. She threw up, squeezed out of the mob, and ran to her hotel room. Desperate to get out of Germany, but needing to go to one more place there, she flew to Danzig, a beautiful medieval outpost. In that city, another speaker blared,

"We belong to the Third Reich! We own the earth. We are unbeatable!"

In the middle of the night, Katya awoke to the sounds of trucks moving back and forth on the street below. Petrified, she watched from her balcony as rows upon rows of German soldiers gathered along the street.

In Poland, the citizens near the German border had begun to evacuate. Fleeing farmers and their wives, children, poultry and a smattering of possessions swarmed onto Katya's train. So did newly called-up recruits—peasants and gentlemen alike. Trapped in the middle of the sea of humanity, Katya could hardly breathe. At the packed hotel in Warsaw, her pre-arranged reservation meant nothing. The manager gave her and dozens of others mattresses in the hallway.

Fear, hatred, despair, and helplessness flashed across the faces of the people of Warsaw, many of them Jews trying to flee the country. The disorderly and poorly equipped, but brave Poles took up as their motto: "Better to die free than live as slaves!"

On August 26, Katya took a train to Lvov, at the eastern border of Poland. Becoming restless and nervous, she wrote,

"I hate war! Where is Nicholas? George? What is happening to my people in Brussels—Canada—USA? Suddenly, I have ceased to be an observer, and have become a human being again, full of personal fears for my own safety. Lord, have mercy on us, the world, and me."

When leaving Lvov, Katya grew jitterier than ever.

"Lord, help me," she wrote. "I am neither worthy to live, nor ready to die."

Two days later, war broke out, with Germany fighting France, Poland, and England.

"Now we are face to face with the result of having left Christ out of the last peace," Katya wrote. Hungry for the sight of a friend, she boarded a train to Yugoslavia, where Nicholas Makletzoff was visiting his brother and sister-in-law.

A few days after her arrival in the city of Ljubljana, Katya and Nicholas left Yugoslavia for France. Nicholas insisted on taking his fishing equipment, "just in case." They reached Milan without trouble, but Mussolini had allied with Hitler, and no trains were going to France.

Thinking fast, Katya spotted a sign in the train station that advertised a train going to a station less than a mile from the French frontier, in the Savoie Mountains. She ran to Nicholas, and told him.

Within seconds, Katya found herself loaded down with not only her own knapsack, but with fishing poles and a tackle box. She bumped and stumbled her way onto the train. Several hours later, Katya and Nicholas got off the in the mountain wilderness. No town or village broke the natural line of the vast landscape.

Standing by the empty track, Katya spotted a lone French outpost off in the distance. She and Nicholas would have to walk to the border.

In the uneven mountainous terrain, Katya tripped over the fishing poles Nicholas wouldn't let her abandon. Every time she fell, he helped her to her feet with a good-natured smile. She glared back, and let him know at full voice, in Russian, French, German, and English what she thought of his fishing equipment.

Katya on her way to Europe

When the French soldier at the outpost cleared Katya, she was so relieved to be on safe soil that she kissed him, and forgot the misery of the fishing poles.

Nicholas, European trip

A frenzied bedlam that had taken hold of Paris shattered Katya's fragile well-being. After a sleepless night in a hotel air raid shelter, she and Nicholas took the three-hour train ride to Brussels.

When it came time to sail for England, Emma went with Katya and Nicholas to the dock.

Katya boarded the boat, and stood at the railing as her mother waved goodbye, smiling and making the Sign of the Cross over her. Realizing she might never see her mother again, Katya leaned against the railing, and wept.

George, at school in England

In England, Katya headed straight to George. She wrapped her arms around him, and nearly fainted when he told her he had begun making plans to travel to Poland in an effort to find her and bring her back to England. And now, at only seventeen, he wanted to return to Canada with her, to join the army. She couldn't persuade him otherwise.

In mid October, when Katya finally got to Grand Central Station in New York City, she found herself in the middle of a joyful mob of children, volunteers, staff workers, and neighbors from Harlem. Their greeting so overwhelmed her that she sat down on the subway stairs and cried. She had been afraid she would never see Harlem or Friendship House again.

Katya and secretary at Katya's desk in FH library

Chapter 25

The Shadow of Darkness

"Even if I should walk through the valley of the shadow of death, I will fear no evil; for Thou art with me."

(Psalm 22/23)

Fr. Paul of Graymoor

*F*riendship House faced possible disaster. Fr. Mulvoy was transferred; and the priest replacing him wasn't much interested in FH or social justice. That was bad enough, but shortly after Fr. Mulvoy's transfer, Fr. Paul of Graymoor died. The loss of her two friends, and the thought of possibly having to close FH, left Katya "filled with sorrow and foreboding." She thought her fears would be fulfilled when Archbishop Spellman called her into his office for the first time since her arrival in Harlem. He surprised her by saying,

"I've followed your work for over two years. It's good. Continue it."

His words and support kept the darkness at bay, until George came to tell her he was ready to sign up for the Canadian army. Canada had already entered the war, and George's news brought Katya's brewing pain to a head. When he left, she adjusted to his peril by tackling a large backlog of work and praying for the millions of other mothers who suffered the same way she did.

George de Hueck, Canadian Armed Forces

"The shadow of darkness is upon us," she wrote. "For years now, I have seen this coming and spoken of it, and written and cried out—'Make straight the way of the Lord'—but who am I that my voice might be heard?"

Katya tried to stick to what she called "the duty of the moment," so she wouldn't get swallowed up by her pain. Seated at her desk one day, she made herself answer a pile of letters. When a shadow fell across the page on which she was writing, she looked up to see a tall man with thick graying brown hair and a mustache in the library doorway. A woman stood at his side. When the man caught her eye, he strode up to her desk.

"This is Helen Worden," he said in a strong, slightly scratchy voice, "and I'm Ed Doherty. We're here to do an article for *Liberty* magazine."

Katya shot to her feet. She punched out her cigarette in the overflowing ashtray.

"You can't peddle that smut here, Mister!" Katya didn't care that her voice carried to every corner of the library. She knew *Liberty* contained plenty of sex and crime; and she didn't want it in Friendship House.

Without blinking an eye, the reporter dropped onto one of the two chairs a volunteer rushed to provide, and kept talking.

"We're here to do an article on the wickedest city in America," he said, pulling out a pen and pad of paper.

Katya glared at him. She lit a fresh cigarette, took a long drag on it, and told the obstinate reporter that if Harlem was wicked, he should go ask City Hall who made it that way.

"Ask the respectable, bigoted Christians of Manhattan and the Bronx, Catholics included. Ask the shopkeepers who fleece the poor!"

Ed Doherty sat fascinated and smitten. This chain-smoking dynamo, with her ink-stained fingers was a dangerous

Edward J. Doherty

beauty—with the kind of beauty that grew and intensified as he watched it.

Ed's first wife had died in the global flu epidemic of 1918. His second wife had died in an accident while on a solitary mountainside walk. He hadn't paid any real attention to a woman since; but the flame in Katya's eyes as she defended the people of Harlem shattered his well-protected reserve. He took care not to let it show. At the same time, Katya's justified anger gave him a great idea. The Harlem story would be good.

As Ed Doherty thought about how terrific the story would be from Katya's perspective, he puzzled over what made her so attractive. Part of the answer, he thought, lay in her compassion.

"No man or woman, white or black," he wrote, "had ever let me see such depths of pity for the poor, the degraded, the ravaged, the swindled, the raped, the exploited, and the trampled on."

Ed produced his checkbook, and made out a donation for Friendship House.

"This is for Blessed Martin de Porres," he said. "I wouldn't have come here if I hadn't seen his name on your window."

Katya's eyes widened as she glanced at the check he handed her. A hundred dollars! Nobody she knew had that kind of money. "Will it bounce?"

Ed smiled. "It won't come back; but I will."

Chapter 26

Eddie

"Not every hero wears a decoration."

(Russian Proverb)

*H*e did.

For some reason she couldn't explain, Katya wanted this man to know Harlem as she had come to know it. She asked Ellen Tarry to give him and Helen Worden a tour, letting them talk with neighbors, local policemen, landlords, and government officials. Sometimes, Katya let Eddie take her out for supper, so the two of them could talk.

Eddie Doherty, second left, with his five brothers, all reporters except for Fr. Marty, priest

After a few months, Katya felt that Ed, who did most of the legwork for the story, had a good grasp of many sides of Harlem. She felt, too, that she had found a friend with whom she could talk about her dreams and hopes for Friendship House.

Ellen Tarry touched on some of those dreams when she wrote in one of her Harlem newspaper articles that, in fighting Communism, FH "held the line in Harlem for the Church until all America, and particularly Catholic America, was awakened to the Communists' design on the African American."

A. Philip Randolph

The time was ripe for spreading the word farther abroad than ever about better race relations. A. Philip Randolph, leader of the Brotherhood of Sleeping Car Porters, proposed a national march on Washington to claim African American entitlement to all the rights guaranteed by the Constitution. He said the only way to stop the march would be for President Roosevelt to issue an executive order forbidding discrimination in industry.

The President did just that.

In his July 25, 1941 Executive Order 8802, President Roosevelt stated,

"I do hereby reaffirm the policy of the United States that there shall be no discrimination in the employment of workers in defense industries or government because of race, creed, color, or national origin."

Mr. Randolph called off the march; and President Roosevelt put together the first President's Committee on Fair Employment Practice. The African Americans of Harlem and all over the country experienced a renewed faith in their government.

With the atmosphere in Harlem relaxing, Katya breathed easier—until George got sent overseas.

"He left for his next step of advancement in the University of Death and Destruction," she wrote to Eddie from Toronto, where she had gone to say goodbye to her son.

About that same time, the departure of some key FH staff workers threw Katya into a further tailspin. The gaps filled in, though; and she recovered. She left at peace for a lecture tour in the Midwest. Eddie drove her from a talk in Milwaukee, Wisconsin, to one in Indianapolis, Indiana.

On December 7, 1941, in the middle of Katya's Indianapolis talk, a nun and Eddie ran onto the stage. The aging Sister said she was a telephone operator, and had gotten the message over the wires that Pearl Harbor had just been bombed by the Japanese.

Eddie confirmed the nun's report.

Katya said to the shocked audience,

"Would everyone stand and join me in singing 'The Star Spangled Banner'?"

Within hours, Katya and millions like her watched in silent anguish as soldiers all over the United States flocked to train stations and airports for deployment.

Chapter 27

Revolutionary Notions

"Katya thought big, worked big, and asked impossible things of other people. Because she inspired them, people often did the impossible."

(Nina Polcyn, Friendship House Staff Worker)

At fifty, Eddie was too old to enlist. But, when Katya read his and Helen Worden's newly published *Liberty* magazine article, she saw that he had entered the battle at home against prejudice.

The first paragraph of "In Darkest Harlem" stated, "Almost half a million human beings eat and sleep and try to live in three square miles. This is Harlem, the wickedest city in the world, created by white men, suffered by blacks."

The article helped place Katya and Friendship House at the forefront of interracial justice. It also inspired an influx of visitors to FH, and created more enemies. Many, in and out of the Church, thought Katya and FH should be silenced. The added stress on Katya's time, resources, and emotions put her on the cross of exhaustion.

Eddie wanted to take Katya down from her cross. He asked his good friend, Auxiliary Bishop Bernard Sheil, to request a Friendship House in Chicago. Eddie lived in Chicago now, and thought that if he could get Katya there, he could protect her better. His added secret hope was to court her at close range.

Bishop Sheil respected Katya and her work. He asked her not only for the house, but to remain single, in order to keep FH alive. When Katya

Reporter Eddie Doherty beside war plane

told Eddie, he groaned. Caught in his own trap. In spite of the adverse development, Eddie thought God was nudging him to marry Katya. He would wait.

Trying to set aside any feelings she had for Eddie, Katya concentrated on the fight against prejudice and injustice. The main weapon she and the members of FH carried had to be love.

"That is all," Katya wrote. "To love the rich and the poor, the friend and the enemy, the good and the bad, the lowly and the exalted. To love God and man. To go on loving when there is nothing left in someone to love. To love all always in God."

She prayed for the strength to detach herself from any personal love that might hinder her in doing God's work.

"Marry me," Eddie said on a regular basis.

"You know I can't," Katya replied every time, and threw herself into her work.

Bishop Sheil asked Katya to send one white FH staff worker and one black to co-direct the new Chicago house. He wanted people to get the picture of an interracial apostolate right from the start.

Katya asked Ann Harrigan and Ellen Tarry to take up the challenge. Both accepted; and Ann asked to do as much as possible on her own, without Katya's presence and help.

With some reluctance, Katya agreed to let her try. But she went ahead with a lecture tour to build up interest and support for the new foundation. In one Midwest lecture, she decried, as always, the Christian complacency that allowed Communism to flourish in the United States. Hecklers at the back caused so much ruckus that Katya had to stop speaking.

Someone called the police, who came and evicted the troublemakers. With them gone, Katya finished her lecture.

Exhausted by all the hubbub, Katya was glad to sit quietly in a taxi with Eddie and ride back to where she was staying. When they arrived, she climbed out of the cab to stand on the sidewalk and wait for Eddie to pay the driver. Suddenly, she was surrounded by a mob of the same hecklers who had disrupted her talk. The rag-

Nicholas Makletzoff, Canadian Reserves

ing women swarmed around her, screaming and yelling. One tore Katya's hat and scratched her face. Another pulled her hair. One grabbed at her coat, and ripped it. It happened so fast, Katya didn't think to defend herself.

The next thing she knew, Eddie appeared at her side. What he said as he peeled the women away from Katya can't be printed here; but his words flew out like shotgun pellets into a bevy of crows. The ladies scattered in all directions, fleeing for their lives.

Over the next while, always thanking God for Eddie, Katya went on with her lecture tour to awaken interest in the new Chicago Friendship House.

At Bishop Sheil's request, she also formed a proposal for an adult education program. Nina Polcyn said Katya "was a great master planner. She had a revolutionary notion of Catholic adult education, with a view toward getting jobs."

Back in Harlem, Katya felt the restless anger of many. She still feared that, because of the injustice done to blacks, there could be race riots, and even a civil war.

Harlem soldiers

Chapter 28

Disappearing Act

"Katya was a storybook character who spoke with zeal and dynamism. She never told a story the same way twice. The story was important, not the facts— never the facts!"

(Ellen Tarry)

Tensions in Harlem quieted down; and Katya went ahead and sent Ann Harrigan and Ellen Tarry to start the new Friendship House Chicago. She came to Chicago, too, to give another lecture.

Katya was clear about one fact. She had to give her whole heart to her work. When Eddie proposed again in Chicago, she forced herself to say they shouldn't see each other anymore. Circumstances helped her resolve. She had to return to Harlem; and the *Chicago Sun* sent Eddie to Iowa to cover a story about the five Sullivan brothers who died at sea when their Navy cruiser was torpedoed in a battle near Guadalcanal.

As much as leaving Eddie occupied Katya's thoughts, she couldn't stop thinking, as well, about Ann and Ellen, who couldn't find a way to get along. Ellen had suffered so much racial prejudice growing up in Alabama that she tended to feel she had to fight and stand her ground before all white people, including Ann. In self-defense, Ann retreated into rigidity and silence.

When Ellen decided to leave Friendship House and pursue a full-time writing career, Katya appointed Ann the sole director of FH Chicago. She named short,

Flewy, second left, and group in FH lending library

Katya, seated middle, Flewy, seated right, with statue of Blessed Martin de Porres in background

blonde, life-loving Nancy Grenell as director of FH Harlem.

"Slowly, yet not completely," Katya wrote, "I allow myself to hope that in Ann Harrigan and Nancy Grenell, the Lord has given me an answer to the question: 'What of Friendship House after I die?' There, within their shining souls, is the continuation of the spirit that made me arise, and walk, in answer to the strange call of God—my vocation."

With Ann and Nancy in charge of the two houses, Katya thought she could spend time writing, lecturing, and developing a Friendship House Training School. Before she could plan a thing, Archbishop Spellman called her into his office. He said Pope Pius XII had asked the U.S. bishops for input on how Communism and the Church affected the lives of young workers of America. Bishop Sheil had suggested that Katya be the one to infiltrate their ranks and find out, because she could blend in with them. Archbishop Spellman stressed the need for secrecy concerning the venture, "so as not to blow your cover."

In her early days as a struggling laundress, the other girls had called Katya Katie Hook. She could become her again—a struggling working girl able to talk freely with all the other workers; but did she want to enter all that desolation again?

After a night and a day of struggle, Katya decided it must be what God wanted her to do. She told the Harlem staff she had to go check out possible locations for new foundations; and disappeared from New York.

Chapter 29

Fifty Cents for the Man

"Christ of the desperate, have mercy on us."
(Katie Hook)

*K*atie Hook emerged from the train station in downtown Chicago. She got a room in an old stone boarding house that seemed more like the "grave of all human hope and decency". She got a job as a waitress in a saloon.

Because of her accent, Katie's fellow workers called her "Katie the Pollack". Grace, a "B" girl in the bar, said something else about her was different, too, something that made her shine.

Katie said that, in God's eyes, Grace shone too, because He cared about her.

"Cares about me? Hah! *Nobody* cares about me."

Katie identified so much with Grace and others like her that she wrote to Bishop Sheil, her contact person, "I keep hoping you will find some way of bringing help to us, the undiscovered home missions of today, the Forgotten Christ who works in a saloon."

The constant boogie-woogie music in the saloon wore Katya out. She left, and drifted from job to job in different parts of the country. Since so many men had left the cities to fight in the war, it was easy for a woman to find assembly-line jobs. While working in a paper-cup-making factory, Katie wrote to Bishop Sheil that the constant clatter of machines made it "a factory version of the boogie-woogie."

Katya as Katie Hook

Besides having to put up with the noise, Katie had to fork over fifty cents to the factory bully, the self-appointed man of all work. He made life hell for whoever didn't pay up.

During the ten-minute break times, Katie and the forty women on her floor stood around a radio, listening to the war news, smoking and talking. Communism sounded good to a lot of the workers. They would have free insurance, they heard, lots of leisure time, and free medicine. The Church couldn't help, they said. It hadn't been there for them yet, so why should they look to it for hope for tomorrow? Now is the time for a revolution.

"Bishop," Katie wrote, "my world of cooks, waitresses, factory girls, porters, dishwashers . . . the same as those who sat and listened in rapture to Christ on the Mount, is crying out for justice and receiving no answer from those who have been sent to give it to them. So they feel like searching for it with kitchen knives and hatchets."

Katya wrote to Fr. Furfey, her current spiritual director and main spiritual guide for FH, to explain where she was and what she was doing.

Fr. Furfey wrote back that he was worried about FH, that it would fail without her.

Katya replied that she would return to New York as soon as possible, but added,

"I beg to go on record that I utterly disagree with the statement that FH will fail if I left or died or got sick.... FH can, and someday will, function without me."

Katya told Fr. Furfey she was sure there would be a cultural revolution in the United States after the War. She said, too, that "the Church, and especially the Hierarchy, priests and nuns, will be persecuted."

In New York, Katya found out that George was expecting at any moment to be appointed to the Canadian Commando Forces. With the invasion of Europe imminent, and the memory of the casualties of the Dieppe raid vivid, Katya could only surrender George to God's protection.

Katya found out, too, that the final papers for a Church annulment from her marriage to Boris had come.

In Beverly Hills writing the screenplay for "The Fighting Sullivans", Eddie made long-distance pleas to Bishop Sheil to allow him to marry Katya.

Because Katya received regular threats resulting from her anti-Communist work, and because many priests attacked her for the stands she took on interracial equality, the Bishop agreed that she needed protection. He said he would consider Eddie's marriage request if he would promise to share Katya's voluntary poverty and always let Friendship House come first for her.

With that added ammunition, Eddie wrote to Katya,

"I'm tired of seeing you 'take it'—tired of remembering your weariness, your worries over this one and that one, your pain, your doubts, your unceasing labors. . . . You can still work yourself half to death and nobody to give much of a damn—except me. But I'll be there to keep you from working ¾ of the way to death."

Worried about how marriage to Eddie would affect the FH staff, the people they served, and the young volunteers who might think she couldn't combine marriage and the running of FH, Katya begged God to show her what to do. After agonized prayer, she wrote to Eddie,

"The night alone heard my slow halting whisper to Him whom my heart loves even more than it loves you."

She told Eddie that the Lord seemed to be asking,

"'Can you serve me as well as you have when your heart is filled with love for one man?'"

For Katya, the Lord then fell silent; and the night held its breath. She finished her letter to Eddie:

"Oh, love of my Russian heart, can I love you and serve God as I must?"

Chapter 30

Lady Pain

"Those who are able to see more deeply know that Love wedded Himself to Lady Pain, and that Love can make her beautiful, as on that day of Love's death."

(Katya: "How Ugly Lady Pain Became Beautiful")

𝒦atya reached a decision; and on June 25, 1943, she married Eddie in a simple ceremony in Bishop Sheil's private chapel in Chicago. The members of Eddie's family served as guests and witnesses—and the only people who knew about the wedding. Katya wasn't ready to face everyone else's questions, criticisms, and opinions.

Katya and Eddie on their wedding day, June 25, 1943

True to his word about sharing Katya's life of Franciscan poverty, Eddie gave away all his possessions and sold his house, giving the money to the poor. The seven dollars a week it took to rent a little place in Chicago at 8 West Walton Place didn't break their personal vow of poverty.

Bishop Bernard Sheil, Eddie, Katya, Eddie's mother, sisters and two brothers

It was a good start for her and Eddie; but Katya didn't get the chance to prove herself with FH before the news of her marriage leaked out. Ann had sensed something in the air, and had called both Eddie and Bishop Sheil to ask why Katya was avoiding her. Their side-stepping responses told Ann all she needed to know. So the very thing Katya had hoped to avoid by not telling anyone about her marriage came about as a result of her secrecy. In the absence of real knowledge, Ann drew her own mistaken conclusions.

"Now she steps out of the picture and leaves me holding the bag—and Nancy the same."

Ann thought Fr. Furfey agreed, and that he now looked to her as the new leader of Friendship House.

Katya did her best to assure Ann, Fr. Furfey, and Nancy that she had no intention of leaving FH. Still,

they didn't seem to understand "a strange wild Russian heart that can encompass the love of a man into the love of God."

"Lady Pain is back again," she wrote. "Why did I think for a moment or two that I ever could shed her—escape the shadow of the Cross."

As much as it hurt Katya to think of FH turning its back on her, she begged Eddie not to say anything.

Eddie reading in boat, Minocqua, WI

"There are so many ways in which I can go on living and working for God—hidden, quiet, humble ways. . . . Perhaps I have been very, very wrong in not telling them. . . . I am ready to pay the price. . . . Let us play the game according to their rules—for always the Common Good comes before the individual one—in this case mine."

Knowing she would have to do something, Katya met with Ann, Nancy, and Fr. Furfey in Harlem. After four hours of painful discussion, she offered her resignation. They refused to accept it, and as she wrote to Eddie,

"We had it out! . . . They saw that my marriage would not interfere—because they finally agreed that I was different— and so were you! . . .

Katya rowing

"I remain Director General. All is well, and my beloved FH has not left me. I am so very happy, darling—and I want you to share it. . . .

"I think it is OK now to let the papers know."

Katya re-started her plans for a Friendship House Training School.

COME·FOLLOW·ME

By Ade Bethune

Cover for Friendship House Training Pamphlet, design by Ade Bethune

"You and I," she wrote to Eddie, "are the heart of a *Lay* Society [in the Church]— A Family. . . . Such an arrangement is ideal because it keeps us so much more together than we were."

The ink from Katya's pen had hardly dried when race riots broke out in Harlem. Lenox, Fifth Avenue, Eighth, and the shopping streets between were left in shambles.

Katya wrote that, "Food, clothing, furniture, department and jewelry stores, laundries, pawnshops, cleaners, drug stores gape, their windows glassless, like big blind eyes, their shelves bare of even ANY memory of merchandise. Sober, grief-stricken owners, with drawn faces, stand silently by—speechless and sorrowful."

Riot squads in white, firemen in red, cops in blue with guns drawn patrolled the streets. Some policemen rode in squad cars; others rode motorcycles. The Army stood guard outside Harlem, making New York "a city under siege." There was no food to be found; and all the liquor was stashed in Harlem basements.

The streets grew quiet; but the fires were only banked.

"There is neither laughter nor gentleness underneath the smooth surface of Harlem lolling, gossiping in the sun. Here and there, a word, a look stabs with swords of hatred—or hangs poised in the air—the arrow of to-morrow's riots.

"Friendship House is untouched—praise the Holy Spirit, Our Mother Mary, and Blessed Martin. Everyone prayed—all night—to the accompaniment of shooting, savage yelling, broken windows. God is good."

As Katya sat in the FH library writing to Eddie, he called from Chicago.

"I heard your voice," she continued in her letter, "and the riots look like nothing at all. What is a riot or two when I am in love—head over heels—with my own sweetheart of a husband?"

In his return letter, Eddie wrote,

"One of the things I love about you—just one of the many things—is that wherever you are there is excite-ment. . . . If nobody makes excitement for you, you make it for them. For me, especially, you have ever been exciting."

Chapter 31

Soldiers' Little Girls Never Cry

*"If you can't bear physical pain, child, how will you
bear the pain of the heart and of the mind that will
certainly come to you?"*

(Katya's father to her when as a little girl she cried after
falling and cutting her knee.)

*H*arlem quieted down again; and Katya decided to go
ahead with plans for a trip to Combermere, Ontario, where Nicholas let her and the FH staff come to
his cabin for rest breaks and training sessions. There
had been times that Katya and Nicholas had spoken of
a possible future marriage. At other times, they drifted
apart and rarely saw each other. Then Katya met Eddie,
and Nicholas met Ann; and life shifted for all of them.
Along the way, Nicholas became a great friend of many
of the other Friendship House workers. He was glad to
provide a place of respite for them.

Eddie, the ultimate city boy, had a different view of
rural life.

"Take care of yourself in that wild country," he told Katya. "Don't get sunburned. Don't over-tire yourself. Don't get eaten by mosquitoes. And don't forget to write a guy."

Katya didn't forget. She wrote to tell Eddie how much the area around Combermere reminded her of the forests of Russia, with their stands of birch and pine trees covering the hills and valleys around the river. She loved going out in the rowboat; and she and Nicholas taught Ann and Nancy how to fish.

After a few weeks in Combermere, Katya arrived in Chicago tanned, rested, and aflame with new ideas for Friendship House. From now on, she said, the head-quarters would be in Chicago. The paper, *FH News*, would be edited there. The training school could be in Combermere or in Marathon, Wisconsin, where Bishop Sheil had given FH the use of a farm.

Fr. Furfey encouraged Katya in her attempts to get the training school going.

"The whole future of the FH movement depends on it," he wrote. "You have put so much of yourself into FH that I couldn't bear to let anything go haywire at this point."

All those plans took place in Katya's conscious mind. On the subconscious level, she had frequent nightmares about Russia's Revolution, the World War now in prog-ress and George's participation in it. She wanted to cry, but her father had taught her from early childhood not to cry when experiencing physical or emotional pain.

"Soldiers' little girls never cry," Eddie heard her say one night in her sleep.

During her waking hours, besides preparing for the training school, Katya worked at balancing the demands of the apostolate with those of married life. As "B", she had to contend with the staff in both Chicago and Harlem starting to "argue every damn point of what seemed to be a settled affair."

As Katie Doherty, Katya nursed poor working neighbors in their homes, scrubbed their floors, cooked their meals and washed their dishes. As she did, she saw "hearts open, and depth, human confidence, and trust flow into my ears. . . . A personal relationship comes in, at which I am most awkward."

In the past few years, Katya had become so used to sending others to attend to people that she had gotten out of practice in doing it herself. As awkward as she sometimes felt, she liked being with people again, and was sure she was doing what God wanted her to do. At the same time, she sensed in Him an expectancy that puzzled her. It seemed as though He had something up His sleeve, but was taking His time in revealing it to her.

Chapter 32

A Broken-Winged Bird

"Hold fast to dreams,
For if dreams die,
You're a broken-winged bird
That cannot fly."

(Langston Hughes)

*W*hile Katya puzzled over what unknown work the Lord might have in store for her, she continued going out to nurse sick neighbors. One lady begged her to go visit a friend in a mental hospital.

"She sits in a corner of her room and won't talk to anyone. The doctor said she's catatonic. They don't know what to do with her."

"I'm a home health care nurse," Katya said, "not a psychiatrist."

"Please, B!" the lady pleaded, using Katya's FH nickname. "If anyone can get through to her, you can."

Katya finally relented. When she got to the hospital, and went to the woman's room, she found her hunched in the corner on the floor, unmoving, staring into space.

"Hello," Katya said softly. She walked slowly toward the corner.

The woman neither moved nor blinked.

Katya sat on the floor beside her, held her hand, and said in a low voice, "I love you; I love you; I love you."

Over the next several weeks, Katya went every day, always sitting on the floor beside the woman and repeating the same refrain over and over: "I love you; I love you; I love you."

One day, the woman's room was empty. Alarmed, Katya ran to the nursing station. As she neared it, she saw a tall, thin woman at the center of a group of nurses. The woman glanced over the nurses' heads, gasped, and shouted,

"It's her! See? The lady in the red dress!"

Startled, Katya took a step backward.

The woman rushed over, and pulled Katya into the circle of nurses. In a flood of words, she told Katya that for what seemed like a very long time, she had been wandering in a deep, dark forest. No matter which way she turned, she couldn't find her way out. The trees drew closer. The darkness deepened. Terrified, she thought if she stayed very still, it wouldn't overtake her. But the darkness kept closing in. She felt lost, alone, and scared.

"Then a lady in a red dress came through the tangle of trees toward me. She took my hand, and, little by little, led me out of the dark forest. And here I am! They say I'll get well quickly now."

Katya wrapped the woman in a bear hug, and went home, where she learned that President Roosevelt had died.

"I loved him, this President of the USA, and servant of Yours," Katya wrote on April 15, 1945. "He helped me to see Your face in high places, where nowadays it is almost never seen."

The following month, Germany surrendered to the Allies. Partial peace had been won. As glad as Katya was, her joy tripled when George got out of the army and came to stay with her and Eddie, to attend the University of Chicago and look for work.

In August, Katya, Eddie, and two staff, Blanche and Belle, went to Combermere for a month's vacation. An unhappy Nicholas greeted them. He was about to lose the land and cabin to someone to whom he owed money. The only way out, he decided, was to keep the smaller island property for himself, and sell the five acres on the mainland, including the house.

Since Katya hoped to make Combermere the location of the training school of Catholic Action, she agreed with Eddie that he should purchase the house with his severance pay from the *Chicago Sun*.

Katya on Nicholas's dock in Combermere, 1946

When Nicholas agreed to the plan, Katya could have danced for joy. In true FH tradition of naming their buildings, she and

Eddie called their new acquisition Madonna House, in honor of Our Lady.

A few days later, on Katya's birthday, she received an even greater gift. The jubilant ringing of bells brought her, Eddie, Blanche, Belle, and a host of neighbors on the run to the little country church.

"The war is over!" a man cried.

Tears and laughter mingled with shouts of joy and relief. The Armistice wasn't signed until a couple weeks later, but truly the end had come.

That same day, Bishop William J. Smith came to visit Madonna House. He gave Katya and Eddie his blessing to use Combermere as a training school and a center for a rural apostolate in the local diocese.

Relieved that the war was over, and thrilled about the training center, but sick at heart over the terrible cost of victory in human suffering, Katya returned to Chicago. Catching up on paperwork, she leafed through some FH diary pages Ann had left for her to see. Tucked between the mundane accounts of daily FH activities, a short string of words leaped off the page and shot into Katya like poison pins. She burst into tears. Ann had written that Katya was incompetent, autocratic, self-willed, dramatic, and highly prone to exaggeration. She questioned if such a person could really be the head of FH.

Wiping away her tears, Katya wrote, "Yes. That is me. Wind pudding and hot air sauce." She thought she had much worse faults than those mentioned; and she was ashamed for getting so hurt by Ann's words.

A harder hit lurked around the corner. In Harlem, Katya learned that Ann and Mabel, the current Harlem Director, planned to overthrow her at the upcoming 1947 annual FH Convention.

When Katya got back to Chicago, Ann and a priest, Monsignor Reynold Hillenbrand, came to see her. They accused her and Eddie of not living up to the standard of FH poverty.

Katya was stunned. Eddie, now out of work, had given his whole previous income to charity. His severance pay had gone for a good cause. Their personal budget was geared to that of a Friendship House staff worker, multiplied by two.

Steeped in pain, Katya wrote,

"The prospect that confronts me is dark, consisting in my imperative need of resigning completely from FH!"

She had long had a sense that God had something as yet unrevealed for her to do, but she couldn't envision life without FH, "the child of my soul."

In her diary, she wrote a prayer:

"Give me the strength to go on working always in Your Lay Apostolate, in that manner that you will desire for me to work."

Fr. Furfey was sure the storm was minor, and that it would blow over soon.

Katya wasn't so sure.

"Either they all trust me—us—or they don't," she wrote to Fr. Furfey. "That is the crux of the matter."

The convention was held in the renovated barn of the Marathon, Wisconsin, farm. The directors and assistant directors of both FH houses attended, as well as a representative chosen from among the staff and volunteers of each house. Four priests came, including Fr. Furfey and Monsignor Hillenbrand.

Katya brought up the idea of Combermere as a place for the proposed Training School. The others said it was too far away from Harlem and Chicago, and too plush.

Katya brought up the idea of starting a Canadian rural apostolate.

"FH began as a broad work," she reminded the other delegates. "It should remain open to other types of work."

"No," the others said. "FH has to remain solely in interracial work."

Ann and the others said FH should be run as a democracy, with a Board of Directors voting on those and other issues.

Katya recoiled. "That would be against the spirit of the mandate given to me by God," she said.

They voted her down. A Board of Directors was formed on the spot. Its members—all except Katya—decided that her term as Director General would be limited to three years, after which the DG would be elected by the staff. They further decided that someone from the board had to be with Katya at all times, to monitor everything she said about FH.

One staff worker there said later, "Everyone started jumping all over B, criticizing and disagreeing with everything she said."

In the face of the rising tide of hostility, Katya remained silent, saying only that they were clearly aiming at her resignation. After the meeting, in the yard between the barn and the house, she said to one of the priests,

"As I would in Russia, I bow low before you and beg your forgiveness. I have been a poor example to the kids. Accept my resignation, and pray for my poor soul."

Since Katya had to have someone from the board monitoring everything she said about FH, she took Ann with her when going to report the convention results to Bishop Sheil.

He erupted like a volcano. "What damn nonsense is this? Throw them out, Catherine. I'll help you recruit another group of people with more sense."

Katya surprised herself by defending Ann and the others. "Let them experiment with doing it their way. If the division becomes public, it could set back faith in the lay apostolate, which is so young and vulnerable. I'll resign, and go to Canada."

"You're the foundress," Bishop Sheil said reluctantly. "If that's what you want, let it be."

When Katya got home, she told Eddie what had happened.

He said, "Maybe God allowed all this to happen in order to make it more and more evident to you, as well as to me, that we should make our headquarters in Canada."

Katya didn't know how she could start all over again in Combermere. She envisioned neighbors and villagers waiting to pounce on her as soon as they saw her coming. Like the woman in the mental hospital, she wanted to huddle in a dark, safe corner where nobody could hurt her.

Chapter 33

The Tomb

*"The tomb
became
the witness
to the
mystery
of the
Victory."*

(Katya: Untitled Poem)

$\mathcal{F}$eeling as though she was entering a dead-end street, Katya perched beside Eddie on an adjacent stool at the counter of Chicago's Russian Oak Restaurant. They were planning their journey "into exile." The sense of doom didn't lift on the trip north, in the big Packard Eddie had borrowed money from Bishop Sheil to buy. The beautiful lakes, pines and birches along the narrow, twisting road to Combermere couldn't fill the emptiness inside her.

When Eddie turned off the main road, and onto a one-lane gravel path, Katya took a deep breath. They had reached their destination. At least, the unfinished six-room house, set back from the road in a small clearing, looked cozy and welcoming. Behind the house, the dazzling blue water of the Madawaska River sparkled in the fresh sunlight of spring. Katya couldn't help but relax a little.

The first thing she saw, when she and Eddie entered the house through the kitchen door, was the table. Set with a red and white checkered cloth, it was laden with homemade sandwiches, salad, and dandelion wine. Water bubbled in the kettle on the wood stove. Maggie Hudson, who took care of the house when no one was there, had prepared their lunch.

Katya and Eddie carried the table and all its contents into the living room, where the wall-length window faced the river.

"Welcome to your new home, Katie." Eddie raised his glass in a toast.

Katya had to smile. Where would she be without Eddie? He and the little house made her feel safe and secure.

The next day, though, when Katya set out to visit a neighbor, her hand shook so much, it took ten minutes for her to push up the latch of the low iron gate. People lived outside the Madonna House grounds. People could destroy her.

In spite of her panic, it didn't take Katya long before she unearthed the types of work that needed doing in the rural apostolate.

A young boy walked seven miles to borrow a book; so Katya started a children's lending library.

Many farmers could grow food for their families, but they had little money for clothing; so, with the help of loyal benefactors, Katya opened a clothing room in the basement.

Katya with her black nursing bag

A middle-of-the-night plea to help a woman about to have a baby inspired Katya to update her nursing degree and start a dispensary. It was a good thing she acted quickly, because soon she could hardly keep up with the nursing calls that tumbled in at all times of the night and day. Nels Boehm, a young man who made extra money running a rural taxi service, often took Katya to deliver a baby or nurse a sick patient. He remembers driving her one night in forty-below-zero weather to an isolated farm. The road ran out; and, wearing her parka and carrying her black medical bag, Katya climbed out of the car. She plunged through the snow up a six-foot drift, and disappeared behind it. Nels wondered if he would ever see her again.

Another night, when Katya walked through a snowy clearing toward Nels's waiting car, she happened to look up and see the stars. Joy flooded her whole being; and after that, the more she went out to the people, the more stars she saw, and the less her hand shook when opening the Madonna House gate.

With home nursing in place, Katya set out to see how the area farmers could get better market prices for their pigs. At the Federal Department of Agriculture in the Canadian capital of Ottawa, she picked up a blueprint of a pigsty for housing and feeding two or three pigs. She bought two young pigs, built the recommended pigsty, and raised the piglets according to the government specifications.

Neighboring farmers laughed at the crazy city woman and her "pig motel".

"Looking after the pigs as if they were primroses!" one man scoffed.

Katya smiled. She had their attention. When market time came, her pigs pulled in the highest prices ever received in the region for yearling hogs. People stopped laughing—and started building their own "pig motels".

"It's like the spiritual life," Katya said. "Example is the best teacher."

Flewy left FH Harlem, and joined them in the rural apostolate. Before a week went by, Katya wondered how they had gotten along without her. Flewy helped cook, iron, sew, and start a vegetable garden. She took over the tedious care and lighting of the cantankerous oil lamps. Most important of all, she fit in well with the local people. Katya's nobility, European background, and Russian accent made her a stranger to many. Simple, straightforward, Canadian Flewy seemed to have been a part of the Madawaska Valley forever. She formed a bridge between Katya and Eddie and their neighbors.

In spite of being an oddity on the local scene, Katya took to life in the country like a frog to a lily pad. With help from a couple neighbors, she planted the apple trees she had gotten from the government. To have an apple orchard like the one she had known as a child in Russia made Katya feel more at home.

To get them through the first winter, Katya stretched their borrowed money as far as possible. She ordered wood for heating and cooking, and bought potatoes and flour. Mrs. Mayhew, from across the road, sold her eggs and milk at a good price. Eddie's heart gave him periodic troubles, but he did the arduous task of pumping water to keep the basement holding tanks filled. In between pumping stints, he wrote books and articles. Katya marveled at the volume of writing Eddie produced, most of which got published and brought in enough money to help keep them going.

Katya at the Madonna House garden gate in Combermere

"We might need money from our writings," Katya said, "but we shouldn't make it our goal for our new Combermere newspaper."

"Agreed," Eddie said. "The goal of *Restoration* should be to tell people about God.

The money for it will come through prayer, begging and donations."

As she nursed, wrote articles for *Restoration,* and worked toward the building up of the rural apostolate, Katya didn't notice, at first, how the numbers of visitors and volunteers increased. When she did realize it, she panicked; and withdrew into what she called "the tomb of my heart." But, she didn't stay there. In time, she built up her courage, and told God she would do her best by those who came. At that moment, the walls of her tomb crumbled.

Chapter 34

A Second Chance

"There is no winter in the land of hope."

(Russian Proverb)

*E*ven though swamped by the affirming waves of guests in Combermere, Katya felt that if she hadn't failed God in some way, the apostolate would still be united. Madonna House, she thought, was God giving her a second chance.

In August of 1948, in Chicago for George's wedding, Katya found out that Ann had married Nicholas Makletzoff in Toronto.

"Leaving FH is not so easy, of course," Ann wrote to Katya, but added,

"Thank you for introducing Nicholas to me (and for a host of other things as well)."

As much as Katya and Ann had disagreed, Katya had never doubted Ann's ability to lead FH USA. She wondered what would happen to it now.

Soon after Katya returned home to Combermere from Chicago, her mother died in Brussels. Katya couldn't afford to go to Belgium for the funeral, and in her diary, she wrote,

"With Mother's death, my whole early life is dying."

Boris had died too, the previous year. Shortly before his death, he had called Katya to ask her forgiveness for all the suffering and pain he had caused her. Katya forgave him, and never spoke ill of him to anyone.

Setting her sorrows aside, she took up the work of an extended lecture tour in the States. At the end of it, she returned home tired and ready for a break. Instead of getting a rest, she had to deal with major personality clashes among the visitors and volunteers.

"Let's close it all down, and go live a normal married life," she said to Eddie.

"Let's wait a while, and pray about it," he said.

Katya sighed, and agreed.

The old story about her being a Communist spy made the rounds again. Seeing the renewed pain it gave Katya, Eddie said,

"Let's forget the whole thing, and go live a normal married life."

Katya smiled. "Let's wait a while, and pray about it."

To accommodate the growing numbers of guests, Katya fed them—and entertained them—by cooking soups and stews in a cauldron over a wood fire in the oversized outdoor grill. She stirred the contents of the big pot with a broom handle, used a shovel to transfer it to pails, and ladled supper into bowls from the pails. All the while, she wondered,

"Where is all this going? Should the staff be connected to FH USA? Should have we a constitution?

What spiritual rudder should I use to guide Friendship House Canada?"

Katya gathered together the scraps of paper on which she had written the words she felt God had given her over the years. She re-wrote the words on one piece of paper, and realized she had the basis of a strong spiritual mandate:

> "Arise—go. Sell all you possess. Give it directly, personally, to the poor. Take up My cross (their cross) and follow Me—going to the poor—being poor—being one with them—one with Me.
>
> "Little—be always little. Simple—poor—childlike.
>
> "Preach the Gospel with your life—without compromise—Listen to the Spirit. He will lead you.
>
> "Do little things exceedingly well for love of Me.
>
> "Love—love—love, never counting the cost.
>
> "Go into the marketplace and stay with Me. Pray. Fast. Pray always. Fast.
>
> "Be hidden—be a light to your neighbor's feet—Go without fear into the depths of men's hearts—I shall be with you.
>
> "Pray always. I will be your rest."

These few words held the essence of her vocation: the call to Nazareth, a simple, hidden, ordinary life shot through with the light of faith. All she had to do was let God show her how to fill in the daily details. She tucked the paper away in her purse, where she could retrieve it whenever she needed it.

Katya lecturing to Summer School group, Combermere

Asking Mary, the Blessed Virgin, to guide her, Katya wrote to Fr. John Callahan, of Rochester, New York, who had recently taught a week at the Madonna House Summer School of Catholic Action. She asked him to be her spiritual director. He accepted; and Katya said, "Now order will enter into my life."

Among other intentions, Katya offered every day for priests. "We desperately need *holy priests*," she wrote.

Early in 1951, Eddie read Katya a letter he had received from a Salesian Father in New York, asking him to write a biography of their founder, St. Don John Bosco. The priest said the Order would pay all of Eddie's travel expenses to Italy to do the necessary research. He also had to do some research in Paris and Lisbon, Portugal, for a novel about Our Lady of Fatima.

Eddie at work in his upstairs den in Combermere

Katya was thrilled. "Will they let you go in October?" She hoped to go to Rome then, for the First World Congress for the Apostolate of the Laity.

"Count on it," Eddie said.

By August, Katya still hadn't received the funds she needed for her trip. She started praying for a miracle.

Flewy said she'd pray too, and added that she didn't feel well. Katya took her to the doctor. He couldn't find anything wrong, and sent her home to rest.

That evening, Flewy felt better. Katya relaxed her guard, and, leaving Flewy upstairs with Dot, her roommate, she went downstairs to visit with Fr. Jim Kaufman, from the States, and with volunteer Phil Larkin.

Eddie and Flewy at a summer fair not long before Flewy's death

A couple of minutes into her visit, Katya heard Dot run across the upstairs hall to Eddie's room.

"It's Flewy! She's dying!" Dot cried.

With Fr. Kaufman and Phil at her heels, Katya raced upstairs. They reached Flewy's room half a second behind Eddie. Katya sent Phil to the parish to get the holy oils from Fr. Dwyer. He returned on the run.

Midway through Fr. Kaufman's anointing, Flewy died.

In shock, Katya went across the road to tell Flewy's dear friends, the Mayhews. When she left them, she wandered into the woods. Vaguely startled when Phil and Fr. Kaufman appeared at her side, she let them lead her home.

The next day, the doctor told them Flewy's death was the result of a coronary thrombosis. It struck like lightning, and had nothing to do with her feeling ill beforehand.

Katya didn't have much time to adjust to Flewy's death. The First World Congress for the Apostolate of the Laity was about to take place. Bishop Smith said he would gladly appoint Katya as a lay representative of the Pembroke diocese, but he couldn't help her financially. Katya kept praying for a miracle of funds. By the end of August, nothing much had happened except that Katya broke a tooth and had to travel the sixty miles to Pembroke to get it fixed.

She and Eddie turned the trip into an outing. After the dental appointment, they went to visit the Omaniques, friends who had brought many donations of clothing, furniture, and money to Combermere.

While visiting in the living room after supper, Mrs. Omanique said they had heard from Bishop Smith that Katya was going to Rome.

"The only graduation present our daughter Mary wants is to go to Europe," Mrs. Omanique said. "We want to give her that gift, but we won't let her go alone. If you'll take her with you, Catherine, we'll get you both First Class boat accommodations."

Katya and Eddie sat speechless before the answer to their prayer for a miracle.

Katya and Pat Keegan, another representative at the First World Congress for the Apostolate of the Laity, 1951, in Rome, Italy

Katya and Madonna House staff worker Mamie Legris at a later Congress in Rome

A Second Chance

Chapter 35

Castel Gandolfo

"Love has wings on its shoulders."
(Russian Proverb)

*K*atya reveled in the wonder of being at the first lay congress in history; but a part of her couldn't settle down. Where was Eddie? He was supposed to have met her in Rome the day before.

Early the next morning, a Sister knocked on Katya's door at the Madams of the Sacred Heart Convent. She said Katya's husband had come to see her. Katya threw on a dress and ran to the parlor. When she saw Eddie she caught her breath. He looked like he'd spent the night out in the rain—which, it turned out, he had. He had lost the convent name and address, and had covered miles on foot, roaming from convent to convent before finding the right one. Several Sisters hovered around the parlor, watching the reunion. For their sake, Katya and Eddie put on a spontaneous drama.

"Edward J., it's about time you got here!"

"Katie." Eddie stepped forward. He bent and kissed her hand. "I was passing by, and thought I'd drop in to say hello."

Katya noticed a kind of fear in Eddie's eyes that wasn't part of their play-acting.

"I had a premonition that something was wrong," he said for only her to hear. "It's all right now."

After breakfast with the Mother Superior, Katya went to the Congress. Eddie left to research material for his book. The next few days, they only met once in a while, on the Via della Conciliazione, where the Congress was being held. In his book, *Cricket in My Heart*, Eddie wrote,

"Always Catherine was surrounded by people who shouted questions at her in various languages. Sometimes she was too busy answering in English, Russian, Polish, German, French, Spanish, or Arabic to talk to me. Sometimes I found a chair and sat at her table. She was always the outstanding personality. She was always the most shabbily dressed. She was always the most alive."

After Eddie left for Turin and Milan to pursue his research, Katya was asked to speak at the labor workshop on social justice for minorities in America. She did her best to give a clear picture, based on her years of experience before and during Friendship House USA.

Not long after her talk, Monsignor Giovanni Battista Montini had her paged. Katya gulped. Why did the Vatican Secretary of State, want to see her? Maybe her labor talk had caused a ruckus among the clergy. By the time she got to the Cardinal's office, she felt weak in the knees.

Monsignor Montini, who would one day become Pope Paul VI, came around his desk and took both of Katya's hands in his. In beautiful French, he said, "I am most happy to welcome you. Please be seated." Grateful to oblige, Katya sat.

Monsignor Montini told Katya that what she had tried to do in Harlem and Toronto was magnificent. He hoped the rural apostolate, so practical and well balanced, would grow.

Katya's jaw dropped. How was it that such a humble apostolate was known in Rome? For the next hour she answered Monsignor Montini's questions about interracial justice and labor in the United States.

At last, seemingly satisfied with her answers, he asked if Katya had thought about the members of her community taking promises of poverty, chastity, and obedience. They could remain a lay community; but the work would be more stable.

His words took Katya by surprise, but she said she would think and pray about it.

"By the way," the Cardinal said, "His Holiness has read your book, *Dear Bishop* (the report made to Bishop Sheil from "Katie Hook"). He wishes to see you, and has granted you a private audience tomorrow morning."

It took Katya a moment to recover. From her infancy, she had learned from her Polish grandmother to love and pray for the Pope. A private meeting with him had never occurred to her as a possibility. She walked out of the Cardinal's office on a cloud.

Crossing St. Peter's Square, she saw a taxi coming at her. Raising her hand, she shouted in English,

"Out of my way!"

The astonished driver stopped.

Katya patted the hood of the taxi, smiled at the driver, and strolled on down the wide avenue. At a sidewalk café, she sat at a small table, ordered a large brandy and a small coffee, and hummed a merry Russian tune.

The next morning, on the fifteen-mile bus ride to the Pope's residence of Castel Gondolfo, Katya had to practice breathing, so she wouldn't faint before she got there.

The Pope's residence had a large high-ceilinged waiting room, with a door opposite the one through which she entered. It looked far away. Katya crossed the near corner of the carpeted expanse to the side of the room, and sat on a red damask-covered chair.

The far door opened; and a slender, ascetic-looking man dressed entirely in white entered the room.

Katya rose to her feet in a daze.

The Pope's white, flat-soled slippers made no sound on the carpet as he came toward her. Long before he reached her, Katya was on her knees, shaking beyond control.

Pope Pius XII smiled, and greeted Katya in French. She kissed his Fisherman's ring, and managed to rise to her feet.

He motioned her to a cushioned chair, and sat in the one next to her. Leaning slightly toward her, he said he had been fully briefed about what she was doing and about the Apostolate. His dark, piercing eyes seemed to look into her soul.

"Madam has suffered much."

Tears rolled down Katya's cheeks. She wiped them away, and heard the Pope say what, to her, were words of life and hope.

"Persevere, Madam, no matter what the cost. Persevere, for on lay apostolic groups like yours depends the fate of the Church and Our Own Person."

Katya groped for words with which to answer him—and found none.

In her silence, the Pope added,

"Have you thought about making your community a more stable one, with promises of poverty, chastity, and obedience?"

Katya replied that she would take his suggestion back to Combermere and present it to the staff.

"Good. And be sure to tell the African Americans that there is tremendous love and pain in my heart for them. I remember them in my daily Mass."

The Pope talked then of the rural apostolate in Combermere, attaching great importance to the way of life of a farmer and the need to preserve that way of life.

He spoke with love about Russia and its people, and said he prayed for them too.

The interview over, Katya knelt; and the Pope blessed her. He added blessings for her blood family and her spiritual family, past, present, and future.

The Pope started to leave, turned back, and said,

"No matter where your apostolate takes you, or what work it engages you in, do not forget the most important unit of society and the church, the family. Do all in your power to help them as a unit."

He took off his white zucchetto (cap) and gave it to Katya. With that, he was gone.

In the bus, on the way back to Rome, Katya thought of the Pope's words, "Persevere, no matter what the cost."

Archbishop McNeil had told her so many years before in Toronto, "If you persevere, your apostolate will cover the world."

At the end of the Congress, Katya left Rome with renewed courage. Her mind exploded with the unlimited possibilities of ways in which Madonna House, and

Friendship House as a whole, could serve God in the Lay Apostolate. Her heart carried another message that she knew she would have to introduce to Eddie. She hoped she would be able to talk with him about it soon.

In Paris, while Mary continued her sightseeing adventures, Katya and Eddie managed to get a few minutes alone at a sidewalk café somewhere along the rue de la Paix. Before Katya could speak, Eddie said,

"What does that radiance in your eyes mean? It's not only because you're glad to see me."

Katya hesitated, and then plunged into her meetings with Cardinal Montini and Pope Pius XII. She saw renewed fear in Eddie's eyes, felt the way he kept looking at the people passing by, pretending to listen to her with mild disinterest. He knew something was coming— something that would affect him as well as her. Something that was connected with his premonition in Rome. She felt for him, but had to continue. Her heart overflowed with a joy she couldn't squelch.

"Pope Pius said people like the FH and MH staff, and you and me, can be lifted up to the status of brothers and sisters by taking promises of poverty, chastity, and obedience, the counsels of perfection! It would make our life and work more stable, while at the same time, we would remain lay people. Isn't that sublime, Edward J.? We, the lay people, wouldn't wear habits. We would dress like always—poor, from the clothing room. We'll need a few rules, but mostly lots of Caritas—real love."

As Katya watched, the fear in Eddie's eyes gradually transformed into glistening joy.

After a long silence, he said,

"We've been given a choice the early Christian martyrs never had. We can give up more than our lives. We can give up each other."

Katya and Eddie looked at each other for a long time in silence; and she realized they had both made a decision. They couldn't ask the members of MH and FH to be celibate and not be themselves.

"It's foolishness doubled and redoubled," Eddie said at last.

"The folly of the cross," Katya replied.

Eddie paid the waiter, and pulled Katya's chair back for her. She stood, and walked hand in hand with him down the street of the Cat That Fishes.

"We have to see how the Combermere staff feel about this new type of apostolate," she said, stepping into a future that would be unlike anything she had yet known.

Chapter 36

Uncharted Waters

"There is no path, no 'way' hewn out for me by predecessors. Hence, it behooves me to rely utterly on God and Mary—while doing my utmost to learn all there is possible to learn."

(Katya: Diary, October 3, 1955)

The air in Combermere hummed with the excitement of becoming a more stable community. As wonderful as that was for Katya, it meant that the time had come for her and Eddie to be united with the rest of the staff in taking a promise of celibacy.

In preparation, Katya moved into her own room. Eddie stayed where he was. Her separation from him turned Katya into a human tornado that pulverized everyone in her path. She fought to get her emotions under control. When she finally succeeded, she apologized to God and all her victims, and thanked them for being patient with her.

Katya and Eddie's death to each other gave way to the life of the Madonna House Apostolate. The main house sprouted a new wing, with a dining room/library downstairs and a chapel upstairs. Nearby, dormitories, offices, and maintenance rooms sprang up. Katya moved to the *izba* on the island, which Nicholas and Ann Makletzoff, who spent almost all of their time in Toronto now, had sold them. The numbers of staff multiplied. New foundations arose in Canada, the U. S., and other countries.

Katya's one big heartbreak was the death of FH USA. Those staff refused the offer to join with FH Canada. Except for the perseverance of a few dedicated staff in Chicago, that part of the historic lay movement died.

In Combermere, the most awesome thing of all, for Katya, was that priests asked to become full-time members of the new community. As daring and innovative as her apostolic dream was, Katya had never had an inkling that priests would be so directly involved in it. Her spiritual director, Fr. John Callahan, became the first full-time priest. Others soon joined him; and the working out of the priests' role in the Apostolate proved to be a daunting task.

"It's hard for them to work with a woman," Katya said, "especially one who, by virtue of twenty-six years in the Lay Apostolate, knows more in the practical and everyday sense about it than they do. Result—tension, difficulties, and increased hostility to me on the psychological level."

Gradually, the new wrinkles got ironed out; but one hot summer day, Katya stepped into a brand new and unexpected wrinkle involving priests in the community.

"I'm going to ask the Pope about my becoming a priest," Eddie said.

Katya tried to "face the whole thing squarely;" but a new loneliness and a deeper sense of exile from her Russian roots settled over her.

Through writing and prayer, Katya adjusted as best as she could to the thought of Eddie's possible ordination. So, she was as stunned as he was when he got a letter denying his request. Although he had taken a promise of celibacy, he was still married; and the Church wasn't ready for married priests. Katya shared Eddie's disappointment. Since boyhood, he had carried a hidden dream of being a priest.

Archbishop Joseph Raya

Then Fr. Joseph Raya, a Lebanese Eastern rite priest, came to visit from his parish in Birmingham, Alabama. He became the first Madonna House Associate Priest; and he told Eddie,

"Don't worry. If I ever become a Bishop, I'll ordain you in the Melkite Rite. We have married priests."

Fr. Eddie Doherty

As usual, God surprised Katya with something she had thought impossible. Fr. Raya became Archbishop Raya of Haifa, Akko, Nazareth and all Galilee. Katya realized her dream of Madonna House becoming a bridge between Eastern and Western Christianity—and Eddie realized his dream of becoming a priest. The new Archbishop ordained him on August 15, 1969, in Nazareth. On Katya's 73rd birthday, seventy-nine-year-old Eddie became Fr. Eddie Doherty.

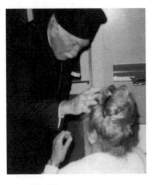

As Katya watched, joyfully and yet with the pain of a detachment she had never yet experienced, Fr. Eddie grew into his priesthood. In spite of his waning health, he celebrated Mass, heard confessions, and traveled between Combermere and the Madonna House foundation in Winslow, Arizona, for the next five years.

Fr. Eddie blessing Katya on his return to Madonna House, Combermere

In mid-January, 1975, Carlos, a doctor-staff worker, called from Winslow to say that Fr. Eddie had a pain in his leg, as well as the old pain in his arm.

A different kind of pain shot through Katya. This could be the end.

Fr. Eddie came to the phone, and said in his gravelly voice,

"I want you to keep our date this evening with 'Cannon.'"

Filled with dread, Katya went upstairs to the priests' den and watched "Cannon", the TV detective program she and Eddie had so often watched together. The scenes floated in front of her eyes, distant and surreal.

On the phone, she had told Fr. Eddie she wanted him home for St. Patrick's Day. He complied. On March 17, he arrived in Combermere in an ambulance. Within days, he had to go to the hospital in Renfrew, sixty miles away. There, on May 4, 1975, he died.

The next few weeks blurred for Katya the way "Cannon" had. On Madonna House's Foundation Day, May 17, she wrote,

"Memories, 10,000, crowd upon me all the time. Eddie promised to make me happy; and he did."

In the fall of that year, Katya wrote,

"We have loved each other so much and so well, darling.

"But we gave it up for the apostolate. Tell me, Eddie, why were we able to do so much for it? In fact, to lay down our life for it? Always reminding each other that we existed 'for the apostolate, and not it for us!'"

In spite of the pain of Eddie's absence, Katya knew she had to continue with her work. In a flash of insight, she realized what God had had in mind for her all along.

Chapter 37

A New Grad Kitezh

"Suddenly, as if a ray of light penetrated my head, my heart, my mind, I knew why I was brought to Canada. Madonna House was going to be a new Grad Kitezh."

(Katya: "Madonna House, What Is It?")

A new what?

Katya gathered the MH staff together to explain that God was calling them to form a place of refuge like Grad Kitezh, the city hidden deep in the forest of twelfth-century Russia. Its citizens had promised to do their best to live by the principles of Gospel peace and love.

"Batu Khan and his 'Golden Horde' murdered all the inhabitants of Grad Kitezh," Katya said, "but they couldn't tear the Gospel foundations of peace and love out of the Russian soul. The hope that Grad Kitezh symbolizes is still alive in the hearts of the people and in the promise that suffering will one day, perhaps only in Heaven, give way to life, joy, and peace.

On the banks of the Madawaska River, a "new Grad Kitezh"

"Like the original Grad Kitezh, Madonna House needs to provide a place where people can come from all over to regain hope or get restored in the atmosphere of God's peace and love."

Some questioned Katya's vision. It took time for them to trust her grace as the foundress of the community. While the spiritual battle between trust and doubt played out, Katya prayed, waited, and, with an aching heart, surrendered it all to God.

Eventually, trust won the battle, and Katya rejoiced that Madonna House was becoming what she felt sure God wanted it to be. It was all right, now, to set her sights on the heavenly Kitezh. One day, in her diary, she wrote to Fr. Eddie,

"More and more I see your face, beloved. More and more I walk Chicago's streets with funny incidents, only I am lame now, and my steps are slow; but my love grows and grows!"

Another day, she wrote,

"Remember, Eddie, how we sat by our river here together—alone, silent and joyful, grateful to God—oh, so grateful! Soon I will join you, my love!"

With Eddie, Katya had laid down her life for the sake of others, enduring the innocent suffering of persecution that had led her to the establishment of a new Grad Kitezh. It had been a great adventure; but the biggest adventure lay ahead.

Pro Nuncio, Archbishop Angelo Palmas,
Katya, Bishop Smith's successor, Bishop
Joseph Windle, at Madonna House, Comb-
ermere

Fr. Eddie Doherty with
Archbishop Joseph Raya

Ann and Nicholas Makletzoff with their
three children

Katya

George de Hueck, who became
a lay minister in the Roman
Catholic Church

Bishop William Smith blessing the newly arrived statue of Our Lady of Combermere

Katya and First Promises group with Our Lady of Combermere: L-R:Clare Becker, Linda Lambeth, Aster Jedynak, JoAnne DeGidio, Theresa Marsey, Joyce Thomasmeyer

Another Promise group: L-R: Fr. John Callahan, First Director General of Priests, Louis Stoeckle, First Director General of Laymen, Katya, Director General of Women and foundress of Madonna House, Tom Egan and Bill Ryan, who have just taken their Promises of Poverty, Chastity, and Obedience in Madonna House Apostolate

Chapter 38

Suffering Redeemed

*"The doors of paradise
have opened for you.
Time has ended.
The moment of eternity has come."*

(Alkonost and Siren, Invisible Birds of Paradise,
The Legend of the Invisible City of Kitezh)

*"I think of death as God's beautiful messenger, bringing me the last love letter of Christ—His invitation
to 'our wedding,' my soul's and His heart."*

(Katya, Diary, November 22, 1955)

*I*n her final years, the early 1980s, Katya entered a new kind of suffering and exile. Due to poor health, she spent time in the hospital and in bed in her *izba* on the island. The staff nurses and other staff took turns caring for her, who had cared for them and so many others for most of her life.

Katya had cried for justice from the rooftops of cities and towns all over the Western world. Badly or well, she had proclaimed the brotherhood of all under the Fatherhood of God. She had accomplished the special work God had asked her to do. Like the pilgrims she had known so long ago as a child in Holy Russia, she had made her own pilgrimage through suffering and pain to a place of peace and love. Now it was time to let God bring her on home to the heavenly Kitezh, and pass on His call to her spiritual children. Her earthly exile was over. She missed Eddie. She longed to see him soon, and meet face-to-face the true Love of both their hearts.

Katya on the bridge to her island *izba*, Combermere

Selected Bibliography

Books

Almedingen, E. M. *My St. Petersburg*, New York: W. W. Norton, 1970.

Benedict XVI, Pope, et al. *Light of the World: The Pope, The Church and the Signs of the Times: A Conversation With Peter Seewald*, San Francisco, Ignatius Press, 2010.

Berdyaev, Nicolas. *The Russian Idea*, Boston: Beacon Press, 1962.

Billington, James H. *The Icon and the Axe: An Interpretive History of Russian Culture*, New York: Vintage Books, 1970.

Borovsky, Victor. *Chaliapin: A Critical Biography*, New York: Alfred A. Knopf; 1988.

Boyle, George. *Pioneer in Purple: The Life and Work of Archbishop Neil McNeil*, Montreal, Quebec: Palm Publishers, 1951.

Brewster, Hugh. *Anastasia's Album: The Last Tsar's Youngest Daughter Tells Her Own Story*, New York: Hyperion Books for Children, 1996.

Briere, Father Emile. *I Met the Humbled Christ in Russia*, Denville, New Jersey: Dimension Books, 1976.

Brown, Kim. *Russia*, San Diego, California: Lucent Books, 1998.

Chaliapin, Fyodor. *Pages From My Life*, New York: Harper & Brothers, 1927.

Curtis, Glenn E., ed. *Russia: A Country Study*, Washington, D. C.: Federal Research Division, Library of Congress; Headquarters, Department of the Army, 1998.

De Hueck, Catherine. *Friendship House*, New York: Sheed and Ward, 1947.

_____. *My Russian Yesterdays*, Milwaukee, Wisconsin: Bruce Publishing Co., 1951.

Doherty, Catherine. *Apostolic Farming*, Combermere, Ontario: Madonna House Publications, 1991.

_____. *Dear Bishop*, New York: Sheed and Ward, 1947.

_____. *Fragments of My Life*, Notre Dame, Indiana: Ave Maria Press, 1979.

_____. *The Gospel of a Poor Woman*, Denville, New Jersey: Dimension Books, 1981.

_____. *Journey Inward*, New York: Alba House, 1984.

_____. *Not Without Parables*, Notre Dame, Indiana: Ave Maria Press, 1977.

_____. *Poustinia: Christian Spirituality of the East for Western Man*, Notre Dame, Indiana: Ave Maria Press, 1975.

_____. *Sobornost: Eastern Unity of Mind and Heart for Western Man*, Notre Dame, Indiana: Ave Maria Press, 1977.

_____. *Strannik: The Call to Pilgrimage for Western Man*, Notre Dame, Indiana: Ave Maria Press, 1978.

Doherty, Eddie. *A Cricket in My Heart*, San Antonio, Texas: Blue House Press, 1990.

_____. *Gall and Honey: The Story of a Newspaperman*, New York: Sheed & Ward, 1941.

_____. *My Hay Ain't In*, Milwaukee, Wisconsin: Bruce Publishing Co., 1952.

_____. *Tumbleweed: A Biography*, Combermere, Ontario: Madonna House Publications, 1989.

Dostoevsky, Fyodor. *The Best Short Stories of Dostoevsky*, trans. David Magarshack, New York: The Modern Library/Random House, 1992.

Dostoevsky, Fyodor. *The Brothers Karamazov*, New York: Farrar, Straus and Giroux, 1990.

Duquin, Lorene Hanley. *They Called Her the Baroness*, Staten Island, New York: Alba House, Society of St. Paul, 1995.

Figes, Orlando. *Natasha's Dance: A Cultural History of Russia*, New York: Henry Holt, 2002.

Gorky, Maxim. *The Lower Depths and Other Plays*, New Haven, Connecticut: Yale University Press, 1945.

Higonnet-Schnopper, Janet. *Tales From Atop a Russian Stove*, Chicago: Albert Whitman & Company, 1973.

Iswolsky, Hélène. *Christ in Russia: The History, Tradition and Life of the Russian Church*, Milwaukee, Wisconsin: Bruce Publishing Co., 1960.

_____. *No Time to Grieve: An Autobiographical Journey*, Philadelphia, Pennsylvania: The Winchell Company, 1985.

Ivoshnikov, Mikhail, et al. *Before the Revolution: St. Petersburg in Photographs: 1890-1914*, New York: Harry N. Abrams, Inc. and Leningrad: Nauka Publishers, 1991.

Kontzevitch, I. M., et al. *The Northern Thebaid: Monastic Saints of the Russian North*, Platina, California: Saint Herman of Alaska Brotherhood, 1975.

Langnas, Isaac A., collector and translator. *1200 Russian Proverbs*, New York: Philosophical Library, 1960.

Lincoln, W. Bruce. *In War's Dark Shadow: The Russians Before the Great War*, New York: The New Dial Press, 1983.

Massie, Robert K. *Nicholas and Alexandra*, New York: Ballantine Books/Division of Random House, 1967.

Massie, Suzanne. *Land of the Firebird: The Beauty of Old Russia*, New York: Simon and Schuster, 1980.

Merton, Thomas. *Seven Storey Mountain*, New York: Harcourt Brace, 1948.

Myers, Walter Dean. *Bad Boy: A Memoir*, New York: Harper Collins, 2001.

Nederlander, Munin. *Kitezh: The Russian Grail Legends*, London: The Aquarian Press, 1991.

Negri, Paul, ed. *Great Russian Short Stories*, Mineola, New York: Dover Publications, 2003.

Neider, Charles, ed. *Tolstoy: Tales of Courage and Conflict*, New York: Cooper Square Press, 1986.

Peck, Richard. *On the Wings of Heroes*, New York: The Penguin Group, 2007.

Pushkin, Alexander. *Boris Godounov*, New York: Viking Penguin Inc., 1982.

_____. *Ruslan and Ludmilla: A Poem*, Moscow: Raduga Publishers, 2000.

_____. *The Tale of Tsar Saltan*, New York: Dial Books/Penguin Books USA Inc., 1996.

Raymer, Steve. *St. Petersburg*, Atlanta, Georgia: Turner Publishing, Inc., 1994.

Sorokin, Pitirim. *Leaves From A Russian Diary—And Thirty Years Later*, Boston: The Beacon Press, 1950.

_____. *A Long Journey*, Lanham, Maryland: Rowman and Littlefield, 1963.

Strickler, Manes E. *Russia of the Tsars*, San Diego, California: Lucent Books, 1998.

Tarry, Ellen. *The Third Door: The Autobiography of an American Negro Woman*, New York: Guild Press, 1966.

Troyat, Henri. *Daily Life in Russia Under the Last Tsar*, New York: The Macmillan Co., 1962.

_____. *Pushkin*, Garden City, New York: Doubleday & Co., Inc., 1970.

Weiss, Pola. *Legends of Russia*, New York: Crescent Books, 1980.

Wild, Robert. *Catherine's Friends: Some Famous People in the Life of Catherine Doherty*, Ottawa, Ontario: Justin Press, 2011.

_____. *Compassionate Fire: The Letters of Thomas Merton and Catherine De Hueck Doherty*, Notre Dame, Indiana: Ave Maria Press, 2009.

_____, ed. *Comrades Stumbling Along: The Friendship of Catherine de Hueck Doherty and Dorothy Day as Revealed Through Their Letters*, Staten Island, New York: St Pauls/Alba House, 2009.

Wilson, Neil. *Russia*, Austin, Texas: Raintree Steck-Vaughn Publishers, 2001.

Wilson, Sandra Kathryn, ed. *James Weldon Johnson: Complete Poems*, New York: The Penguin Group, 2000.

Wintz, Cary D., ed. *Harlem Speaks: A Living History of the Harlem Renaissance*, Naperville, Illinois: Sourcebooks, Inc., 2007.

Woodridge, Connie Nordhielm. *The Brave Escape of Edith Wharton*, New York: Clarion Books, 2010.

Yarmolinsky, Avrahm, ed. *The Poems, Prose and Plays of Pushkin*, New York: The Modern Library, 1936.

Ziegler, E. Charles. *The History of Russia*, Westport, Connecticut: Greenwood Press, 1999.

The Editors of Time-Life Books. *What Life Was Like in the Time of War and Peace: Imperial Russia AD 1696-1917*, Alexandria, Virginia, 1998.

Magazine and Newspaper Articles

De Hueck, Catherine, "Baroness Jots It Down," *Friendship House News*, June, 1943.

De Hueck, Catherine, "Flewey, Alias Contessa Flewjinski," *Friendship House News*, July-August, 1943.

De Hueck, Catherine, "Rendezvous With Christ," *The Catholic Life*, December, 1939.

De Hueck, Catherine, "St. Francis Comes to Harlem," *The Lamp*, June, 1938.

De Hueck, Catherine, "Saint Over Harlem [Blessed Martin de Porres]," *The Torch*, June, 1941.

De Hueck, Catherine, "Three Days in Danzig," *Commonweal*, September, 1939.

Doherty, Catherine, "A Day in Friendship House," *Lamp*, Vol XXXIV, #2, pp. 56-57, Feb. 15, 1936.

Doherty, Eddie, "Harlem Madonna," *St. Anthony Messenger*, April, 1944.

Doherty, Eddie, et al., "In Darkest Harlem," Two-Part Article; *Liberty Magazine*, January 3 and 10, 1942.

Kulikovsky-Romanoff, Olga, "To Be and Not to Seem: My Mother-in-Law, Grand Duchess Olga Alexandrovna: An Interview with Olga Nikolaievna Kulikovsky-Romanoff," *Road to Emmaus*, Vol. III, No. 4, pp. 2-33, Fall 2002.

Tarry, Ellen, "Baroness Cries Peace on Return to Harlem," *Amsterdam News*, October, 1939.

Grand Duchess Olga Alexandrovna, "1919, A Refugee Christmas," (letters from Grand Duchess Olga Alexandrovna to her mother,) *Road to Emmaus*, Vol III, No. 4, pp. 34-47, Fall 2002.

Raymer, Steve, "St. Petersburg: Capital of the Tsars," *National Geographic Magazine*, Vol. 184, #6, pp 96-121, Dec, 1993.

"The Christmas Vigil," *Road to Emmaus*; Vol. III, No 4, pp. 69-71, Fall 2002.

"The Greatest War of All Time Has Come to an End," *San Antonio Evening News*; Vol. 1, #56, San Antonio, TX; November 7, 1918.

Restoration, Madonna House Apostolate monthly newspaper, many and varied articles from 1947 to 2012.

Opera:

Rimsky-Korsakov, Nicolai, and Vladimir Belsky, *The Legend of the Invisible City of Kitezh and the Maiden Fevronia: Opera in four Parts*, St Petersburg, Russia, 1905.

Interviews (Oral History)

Bates, Belle/Lorene Duquin; October 22, 1994.

Cantwell, Fr. Dan/Lorene Duquin; September 21, 1992.

Davis, Theresa/Fr. Émile-Marie Brière; May 21, 2004.

De Hueck, Anatole/Lorene Duquin; December 9, 1990.

De Hueck, Anatole and Doris/Lorene Duquin; January 19, 1991.

Field, Beatrice/Fr. Ric Starks; July, 1979.

Field, Joyce/Lorene Duquin; June 12, 1993.

Furfey, Fr. Paul Hanley/Lorene Duquin; April 10-11, 1991.

George, Réjeanne/Echo Lewis; January 18, 2011.

Guinan, Jim/Lorene Duquin; September 1, 1993.

Mayhew, Julia/Fr. Émile-Marie Brière; November 28, 1977.

McTernan, Fr. Fred/Echo Lewis; February 23, 1981.

Patenaude, Laurette/Echo Lewis; February 24, 2011.

Tarry, Ellen/Lorene Duquin; March 3, 1991.

Lecture Typescript

De Hueck, Catherine, "The Dynamite of Christianity Can Out-Dynamite the Dynamite of Communism", January, 1939.

TV Special

"Russia: Land of the Tsars" History Channel, May 26 and 27, 2003.

Web Site

Kai Kracht, 2002: http;/www.kaikracht.de/balalaika/English/songs/"Dubinushka".

Unpublished or Privately Published Material

De Hueck, George, ed., *Family Notes: A Journal of the Hueck Families*.

Doherty, Catherine, *Diaries*, 1918 – 1981.

Doherty, Catherine, *History of the Apostolate: 1930-1963*.

Doherty, Catherine, *In One Ear and Out the Other: Stories for Staff Workers*, Madonna House Archives.

Doherty, Catherine, *The Little Mandate: How It Came to Be*, M# 603; Band 1-3; April 27, 1968.

Doherty, Catherine, *Staff Letters: 1956 – 1983*.

Kolyschkine, Serge, "Years 1895 – 1903", from his *Unpublished Family History*.

Vishnewski, Stanley, *The B Goes to Harlem*.

Picture Credits

Photos and graphics, except for those indicated below, are courtesy Madonna House Archives and Madonna House Publications, or are in the Public Domain.

Page 14: "Granny—a 'Babushka'". Reprinted with the permission of Scribner, a Division of Simon & Schuster, Inc. from *Invisible Threads* by Yevgeny Yevtushenko. Copyright ©1981 by Yevgeny Yevtushenko. All rights reserved.

Page 19, 20, 22: Bob Staib. Reprinted by permission.

Page 21: © Альфа-Колор, Санкт-Петербург 2003. Permission requested.

Page 47: "A Secluded Monastery", Vitaly Linitsky. ©Keston College, P.O. Box 752, Oxford OX1 9QF Heathfield Road, Keston, Kent BR2 6BA. Used with permission.

Page 47: Basilica of St. Basil, Hand-colored lithograph by Alphonse Bichebois, c. 1850. ©Metropolitan Museum of Art, Bequest of Alfred Duane Pell. Permission requested.

Page 54: WA1949.331 Ivan Yakovlevich Bilibin, Design for the Décor of 'Grad Kitezh' ©Ashmolean Museum, University of Oxford. Reprinted by permission.

Page 80: Claude McKay, http://www.marxists.org/glossary/ people/m/ pics/mckay-claude1.jpg

Page 80: Langston Hughes, used with permission of Van Vechten Trust.

Page 115: Fr. Michael Mulvoy, St. Francis of Assisi University Parish, University of Alabama, Tuscaloosa, Alabama, http://www.stfrancisuo-fa.com/index.php?page=about-us. Used with permission.

Page 134: A Philip Randolph, http://esllevelthree.blogspot. ca/2010/06/great-american-labor-leaders-from-voa.html

Page 191: George deHueck, by Ilinca deHueck. Used with permission.

Books by Catherine Doherty

Available through Madonna House Publications

Apostolic Farming
Beginning Again: Recovering Your Innocence through Confession
Bogoroditza: She Who Gave Birth to God
Dear Father
Dear Seminarian
Dearly Beloved: Letters to the Children of My Spirit (3 Vol.)
Donkey Bells: Advent and Christmas
Fragments of My Life
God in the Nitty-Gritty Life
Grace in Every Season
In the Footprints of Loneliness
In the Furnace of Doubts
Light in the Darkness
Living the Gospel Without Compromise
Molchanie: The Silence of God
Moments of Grace (perpetual calendar)
My Russian Yesterdays
Not Without Parables: Stories of Yesterday, Today and Eternity
On the Cross of Rejection
Our Lady's Unknown Mysteries
People of the Towel and Water, The
Poustinia: Encountering God in Silence, Solitude and Prayer
Re-Entry Into Faith
Season of Mercy: Lent and Easter
Sobornost: Unity of Mind, Heart and Soul
Soul of My Soul: Coming to the Heart of Prayer
Stations of the Cross
Strannik: The Call to the Pilgrimage of the Heart
Uródivoi: Holy Fools

Some books available in electronic format at
www.madonnahouse.org/publications